5 Women Who Love Lesbian Lists, and What They Each Say About It

1. ANN BANNON, author of the Beebo Brinker series
   "This book will interest you and inform you, but more than that it's fun. Everyone will talk about it and you should have a copy. Enjoy!"

2. LYNN LAVNER, entertainer
   "For sheer fascination, this book is at the top of my list. Don't try to be a lesbian without it."

3. GRETA SCHILLER, director of *Before Stonewall*
   "This book is great fun, for the history buff and for anybody interested in a sort of 'who's who' of international pre-Stonewall lesbian life."

4. JUDY GRAHN
   "Dell Richards's massive gathering of information makes it clear that we have a culture of our own, with its own political history, its own philosophy, and its own cosmology. Works like this also make it all the more likely that there can be lesbian studies programs to maintain this public voice."

5. LEE LYNCH, author and columnist.
   "I started reading *Lesbian Lists* for fun. Then it dawned on me: this book is a resource and a validation. We can never record too many facts about lesbian culture; the act of listing is one of handing down, of passing on, a joyous *we are!*

LESBIAN LISTS

A look at lesbian culture, history, and personalities
by
DELL RICHARDS

Boston : Alyson Publications, Inc.

This is a paperback original from Alyson Publications, Inc.,
40 Plympton St., Boston, Mass. 02118.
Distributed in England by GMP Publishers.

First edition, first printing, January, 1990.

ISBN 1-55583-163-X

Library of Congress no. 89-083306

Contents

Switch-Hitters and Cross-Dressers

Lesbians and the Law

A Global Affair

For JEANNINE,
who almost had a
nervous breakdown

Acknowledgments

A book of this magnitude wouldn't have been possible without the help of many people — friends and colleagues, acquaintances, and even strangers. Nor would it have seen the light of day without the many scholars whose work is laying the foundation of lesbian and gay history.

First of all, I would like to thank Leigh Rutledge whose own work, *The Gay Book of Lists*, inspired mine.

Second, I would like to say how indebted I am to the scholars whose research was the basis of so many lists. Their books are listed in the section "For Further Reading." They are Lillian Faderman, Brigitte Eriksson, Janice Raymond, Susan Cavin, Judith Schwarz, Jonathan Katz, Vito Russo, Kaier Curtin, Helen Diner, Rudolf Dekker, Lotte van de Pol and Louis Sullivan.

Third, I would like to thank friends like Annie Woodhouse, Joyce Bright, Theresa Corrigan, Tee Corinne, and Linda Birner, for sending me packages of information and letting me run wild with their books and photocopiers.

Fourth, I would especially like to thank people not mentioned in the text who took the time to send lists: Judith Schuyf, Louis Gooren, Annabel Faraday, Renée van de Giessen, Kate Weiss, Jen Rydstrom, Liz O'Lexa, and Barbara Gittings.

Special thanks is owed to two people who sent extensive information: Michael Willhoite and Keith Clark, both of whose delightful letters were a joy to receive and read. Also, Carol Seajay and Bruce Bates read the manuscript and provided valuable comments.

I would also like to thank those people who provided me with information that allowed me to go forward — such as Sue Hyde of the National Gay and Lesbian Task Force, among many others.

I will also be forever indebted to the gay and lesbian press not only for the detailed coverage it gives to the lesbian community — which provided me with much of the information — but also the editors and writers I work with who provided specific leads and entries: Sabrina Sojourner, Tracy Baim, Alison Brooke, Cliff O'Neill, Susan Lumenello, and Cookie Andrews-Hunt.

Last but not least, I would like to thank Sasha Alyson for thinking of me.

—Dell Richards

Introduction

Two questions haunted me in compiling the lists for this book.

First, how should I define a lesbian? Should I use a contemporary, twentieth-century definition? And if so, which one? Women who are sexually attracted to other women or women who became lesbians through feminism? Or should I use a much broader definition, one that includes the romantic friends movement — women who were women-identified, who had affectionate and loving relationships with other women but may not actually have had sex due to the repressive nature of the era? Should I include sworn sisters and berdaches? Should I include transvestites? Should I include spinsters?

For me, becoming a lesbian was a conscious political decision, the logical extension of feminism. Perhaps it was silly but I took the slogan "Feminism is the theory; lesbianism the practice" to heart and became a lesbian on the heels of becoming a feminist. The question of why I became gay is central to my answer.

Virginia Woolf said that women reflect men twice their natural size. What she didn't do was finish the sentence: Men reflect women *half* their natural size. When I became a feminist, I began to see how distorted the heterosexual mirror was. I decided to see what I would be like in a mirror that reflected me at my natural size. The only way I could think to do that was by ridding my life of men — or at least ridding my personal life of heterosexual men.

While the transition was harder than I expected, the experiment was a great success. Although society sets up a myriad of unnecessary barriers that lesbians constantly come up against, being a lesbian has changed my sense of self in ways I never imagined possible. I honestly believe I see myself today in a much more realistic mirror than I did with heterosexual eyes. I certainly take myself more seriously and give myself more credit as a person and a writer than I used to — and I believe that much of this growth has come from having women — and gay men — in my life, people who believed in me, wanted to see me succeed, and were willing to support me emotionally and professionally in that struggle.

My own bias is toward women-identified women, whether they call themselves lesbians or not, whether they had sex or not. To impose today's standards on earlier eras limits our vision and our history. To dismiss romantic friends, spinsters, and sworn virgins, the women who have done everything in their power to escape heterosexual dominance, does them — and us — a grave disservice.

Given that times change and the perception of reality changes with those shifts, I chose as broad a definition as possible — one that would include a woman-oriented view of the world as the basis of lesbianism.

But that left yet another question, which unfortunately wasn't answered as easily as the first. If a woman didn't say she was a lesbian, how could I be sure?

As a journalist trained to go directly to the source and ask, the answer was one I'm not used to: I had to take other authorities and other sources on faith. With the exception of Amazon forebears like Renée Vivien and Natalie Barney or women like George Sand who enjoyed scandalizing the bourgeoisie, few women-loving women ever publicly said they were gay before 1970. Even the word "lesbian" is a recent invention. Prior to the twentieth century, it meant someone from the isle of Lesbos. And lesbians were called "Sapphists" or "tribades" — if they were called anything at all. For the most part, women who loved women weren't called anything — they were ignored by society, scholars, and history.

To compile the lists, I found that I had to go on clues — tantalizing clues gleaned from shreds of evidence but clues nonetheless. Few women left autobiographies, letters, or diaries that gave explicit answers. Even if they did, the work was often destroyed upon their death, at their own request or otherwise, by lovers, friends, or relatives.

Even women writers who left literary records of their lives usually disguised their sexuality. Gertrude Stein wrote in code; Amy Lowell changed the "she" to "he"; Willa Cather wrote stories with herself as a male protagonist.

If the women didn't change the words, their editors did so, to make the work "universal" — more palatable to a heterosexual audience. Until the 1920s, even Sappho's poems were edited into heterosexual metaphor.

When it comes to sweeping lesbian under the carpet, critics and scholars — the ones who like to present themselves as unbiased as scientists — have been the worst offenders. Instead of shedding light, they have been the first to cover it up.

As late as 1971, Patricia Meyerowitz wrote that Gertrude Stein and Alice B. Toklas were only friends. They made a home together and had an emotional bond that held them together, she admitted, but "lesbians never."

Certainly Gertrude and Alice didn't flaunt their lesbianism the way Natalie Barney did. All the same, they had one of the most traditional marriages of all time. Stein asked Toklas to marry her and promised to support them. When they were running low on funds, Toklas reminded Stein of that promise. Stein's first major success, *The Autobiography of Alice B. Toklas*, apparently grew out of that responsibility.

At their famed salon, Stein entertained the men with literature while Toklas shunted the wives off to the kitchen to talk servants and recipes. In fact, Stein played the male role to an incredible extent. She even cropped her hair so short she was said to look like a Roman emperor.

Stein and Toklas were not bohemian but conservative, by most standards. But if this flaming butch-femme pair weren't gay, then the word "homosexual" has no meaning.

The problem of invisibility becomes even worse if the woman was married — as most women were until the relative economic parity and freedom of the last few decades.

Iris Butler, a biographer of Sarah Churchill, the Duchess of Marlborough, goes to great lengths to downplay Sarah's long-term love relationship with Queen Anne. Butler describes the happy marriages of both the women; then, mentioning the rumors of romance that have persisted over the centuries, she says they can't possibly be true. Queen Anne simply had a weak personality — she always relied on a female companion for emotional support and political advice.

Yet not a chapter further, the biographer's blinkered vision lands her in hot water. Prior to the final break between the two, they had a fight on the steps of St. Paul's Cathedral that was so emotional not even the presence of hundreds of spectators deterred them from screaming at each other at the top of their lungs. Butler calls the event "unexplainable" but it's easily explained if we see that the two women were in love, had been for years, and were breaking up. Sarah was being replaced by her own cousin — a woman she had introduced to Anne — and a battle royal ensued. During it, Sarah — a mere duchess — had the gall to shout at the queen, in public no less. It was shocking for a mere "subject" but not so shocking for old flames.

As long as women are economically dependent and heterosexuality is the dominant mode, lesbianism will be shoved into the closet. And those of us searching for roots will have to be willing to put together clues to create a whole picture. We will have to go on hints, on innuendo even, to find the truth. But lesbians have existed throughout time and will continue to do so — in one form or another — whether hidden or not.

I have tried to present lesbianism in all its wonderful diversity, in varieties that span the globe and the centuries. However the women defined themselves, however we might define them, has not been as important to me as the fact that they were part of the struggle for women's freedom and a lesbian-feminist continuum that has existed for thousands of years.

Because of space limitations, I have concentrated on lesbians prior to 1970, prior to the Stonewall riots and the National Organization for Women's resolution supporting lesbianism. Lists that included the whole spectrum of contemporary lesbianism — authors, photographers, and artists — would have filled volumes. Occasionally I have made exceptions where lesbian history still needs to be fleshed out, as is the case with contemporary lesbian theorists. It is a way of showing what the courage and economic freedom of the past few decades have accomplished — creating not only careers but a separate and distinct lesbian culture.

Although much research has already been done, the search for names and the struggle to create a full and vibrant history of lesbianism is still in its infancy. Most lesbians — like most people — lead quiet lives. They work and play without creating controversy, without catching anyone's attention.

Most of the women in this book weren't like that. They didn't want to be invisible, or for some reason couldn't be. As a result, they have come to someone's attention and been brought to light. In other words, the women in this book are a very select few. They are the tip of the iceberg.

I have met and have known ... a long galaxy of great women ... those older women have gone on, and most of those who worked with me in the early years have gone on. I am here for a little time only and then my place will be filled as theirs was filled. The fight must not cease; you must see that it does not stop.

—Susan B. Anthony

LESBIAN LISTS

Arts and Lettres

19 Lesbian Novelists

1. CHRISTA WINSLOE, d. 1944, France

Winsloe wrote the novel *The Child Manuela*, which is best known today as the basis for the movie *Mädchen in Uniform*. Although Winsloe married, for a time she and journalist Dorothy Thompson were lovers; Winsloe came to the U.S. with Thompson during World War II. Upon returning to Nazi-occupied France, Winsloe was murdered on the street by a common criminal.

2. VIOLET PAGET, b. 1856, France

Though forgotten today, Paget wrote many novels under the name "Vernon Lee" and had a Boston (i.e. lesbian) marriage with Kit Anstruther-Thomson.

3. MARIE CORELLI, 1855-1924, England

Corelli was called "The Queen of the Best Sellers"; her turn-of-the-century romantic novels outsold all other books of the day. Her lover was Bertha Vyver; Vyver edited Corelli's memoirs, *Memoirs of Marie Corelli*, published in 1930. In the relationship, Bertha was "Mamasita" and Marie "Little Girl." Corelli was the pen name of Mary Mackay.

4. FLORENCE CONVERSE, b. 1871, U.S.

In 1897 Converse wrote *Diana Victrix*, which glorifies women who remain single and are romantic friends. She had her own romantic friendship with Vida Dutton Scudder of Wellesley.

5. WILLA CATHER, 1873-1947, U.S.

Cather's most famous work is *Death Comes to the Archbishop* but she portrays herself as the male protagonist in the novel *My Ántonia*. She received the Pulitzer Prize in 1923 and had a Boston marriage with Edith Lewis.

6. GALE WILHELM, early twentieth century, U.S.

Highly acclaimed in her day, Wilhelm's five novels, published in the decade between 1935 and 1945, include two with lesbian characters: *Torchlight to Valhalla* and *We Too are Drifting*.

7. BRYHER, 1894-1983, England
Born Winifred Ellerman, Bryher nursed poet H.D. back to health after her disastrous marriage and pregnancy. Their many years together are chronicled in Bryher's autobiography, *The Heart to Artemis*.

8. GERALDINE JEWSBURY, nineteenth century, England
Her novel, *The Half Sisters*, is about lesbian actress Charlotte Cushman.

9. DJUNA BARNES, 1892-1982, U.S.
Called a creator of modern literature, Barnes was in Paris during its lesbian heyday although she was not particularly enamored of the Natalie Barney circle, which she satirized in *The Ladies Almanack*. *Nightwood* is her most famous work.

10. ISABEL MILLER, b. 1924, U.S.
Miller's novel *Patience and Sarah* details the Boston marriage of Patience White and Sarah Dowling, who lived on a New York farm together in the early nineteenth century.

11. DAME IVY COMPTON-BURNETT, 1884-1969, England
During her life, Compton-Burnett wrote seventeen novels, many of which detail upper-class England at its worst. She lived with Margaret Jourdain, an antique scholar and collector, for nearly thirty years. Their relationship could probably best be called a "romantic friendship"; it apparently did not include sex.

12. SYLVIA TOWNSEND WARNER, early twentieth century, England
Townsend Warner wrote poetry as well as novels, including the well-known *Whether a Dove or a Seagull*, with lifelong companion, Valentine Acklund, whose 135-page love letter to Sylvia was published in 1985 as *For Sylvia*.

13. ANNA BLAMAN, 1905-1960, Netherlands
Blaman wrote the first lesbian novel published in the Netherlands. It became a "succès de scandale" in 1948.

14. MARGUÉRITE YOURCENAR, 1903-1987, Belgium
Yourcenar was the first woman named to the prestigious Académie Française. Her most famous novel is *Hadrian's Memoirs*, about Hadrian and his male lover, Antinoüs. Her lifelong companion was Grace Frick.

15. VIOLETTE LEDUC, b. 1907, France
Leduc's lesbian novel, *Thérèse et Isabelle*, was published in 1967; her autobiography, *La Bâtarde*, in 1965.

16. EDITH SIMCOX, b. 1894, England
Today, much of Simcox's work is forgotten. She is probably best known now for her unrequited "affaire de cœur" with novelist George Eliot.

17. MARY RENAULT, 1905-1983, France
Born Mary Challans, Renault is best known for her historical romances about gay men. But her novel *The Middle Mist* has a lesbian theme. She lived with Julie Mullard for most of her life.

18. MONIQUE WITTIG, b. 1935, France
Wittig's first novel, *The Opoponax*, won the prestigious French award, the Prix Médicis. Two lesbian novels, *Les Guérillères* and *The Lesbian Body* also won critical acclaim.

19. GERTRUDE STEIN, b. 1874, U.S.
Although born in Pennsylvania, Stein resided in Paris for all of her adult life with her companion, Alice B. Toklas, about whom Stein wrote her most famous book, *The Autobiography of Alice B. Toklas*. Stein was also known as a patron of the arts for her literary salons and her collection of early modern painters such as Picasso.

5 Famous Bisexual Novelists

1. GEORGE SAND, 1804-1876, France
Born Amandine Aurore Lucie Dupin, Sand later became Baronne Dudevant. Married and bisexual, she created a sensation by wearing men's clothes, smoking cigars in public, and having affairs with women. Her novel *Lélia* also created a scandal for its eroticism.

2. COLETTE, 1873-1954, France
Sidonie Gabrielle Claudine is most famous for her *Claudine* series, set in a French girls' school. The novel *La Vagabonde*, however, is of more interest to lesbians; it tells about the years after Colette's divorce when she was involved with "Missy", the ex-wife of the Marquis de Belbeuf and daughter of the Duc de Morny. During this time, Colette cropped her hair, wore English ties, and sported a bracelet engraved with the phrase, "I belong to Missy." She was awarded many honors during her lifetime and in 1945 was chosen for the Académie Goncourt.

3. KATHERINE MANSFIELD, 1888-1923, New Zealand
Mansfield spent much of her life in England and her most famous work, *Prelude*, was the first book published by Virginia Woolf's Hogarth Press. Mansfield reportedly left her first husband one day after their marriage.

4. ELIZABETH BOWEN, 1899-1973, Ireland
Bowen, too, spent much of her life in England, writing over ten novels and seventy short stories. Her last novel, *Eva Trout*, won the James Tait Black Memorial Prize in 1969. She was part of Virginia Woolf's literary circle.

5. ANAÏS NIN, 1903-1977, France
Nin lived most of her life in Paris and is perhaps most famous for her extensive journals. In the 1936 novel *House of Incest*, she created the widely-repeated image of lesbian love as a mirror of self.

6 Authors Who Were Lesbian or Used Lesbian Themes

1. SARA JANE CLARKE, b. 1840, U.S.
Part of lesbian actress Charlotte Cushman's circle, Clarke wrote novels and journalism under the name of "Grace Greenwood."

2. MARY HALLOCK FOOTE, b. 1847, U.S.
A well-known illustrator and Western writer, her love letters to "Helena" were only recently discovered.

3. MARIA GRAHAM, d. 1842, England
A bluestocking, Graham was intimately involved with Maria Leopoldina, empress of Brazil.

4. ELIZABETH CRAIGIN, fl. 1937, U.S.
The novel *Either is Love* documents two loves — one for her husband and one for a woman — with equal fervor.

5. JO SINCLAIR, twentieth century, U.S.
Her 1946 novel *The Wasteland* includes a very human and compassionate portrayal of a lesbian.

6. MARY CONSTANCE DUBOIS, b. 1879, U.S.
Many of her short stories, such as *The Lass of the Silver Sword*, have strong women figures and lesbian overtones.

12 of the Most Important Works of Lesbian Fiction Written before 1984 *

1. RADCLYFFE HALL, *The Well of Loneliness*, 1928

2. DJUNA BARNES, *Nightwood*, 1937

3. CLAIRE MORGAN, *The Price of Salt*, 1952

4. JANE RULE, *The Desert of the Heart*, 1964

5. ISABEL MILLER, *Patience and Sarah*, 1971

6. RITA MAE BROWN, *Rubyfruit Jungle*, 1973

7. MONIQUE WITTIG, *The Lesbian Body*, 1975

8. ELANA DYKEWOMON NACHMAN, *Riverfinger Women*, 1974

9. JUNE ARNOLD, *Sister Gin*, 1975

10. BERTHA HARRIS, *Lovers*, 1976

11. SALLY GEARHART, *The Wanderground*, 1978

12. AUDRE LORDE, *Zami: A New Spelling of My Name*, 1983

*This list was compiled by Bonnie Zimmerman, Chair of Women's Studies Department, San Diego State University and author of *The Safe Sea of Women: Lesbian Fiction 1969-1989*, forthcoming from Beacon Press.

20 Twentieth-Century Works with Lesbian Themes Published by Mainstream Houses

1. *THE PURE AND THE IMPURE*, Colette, Farrar (1933)

2. *THE AUTOBIOGRAPHY OF ALICE B. TOKLAS*, Gertrude Stein, Harcourt, Brace (1933)

3. *WE TOO ARE DRIFTING*, Gale Wilhelm, Random House (1935)

4. *NIGHTWOOD*, Djuna Barnes, Harcourt, Brace (1937)

5. *TORCHLIGHT TO VALHALLA*, Gale Wilhelm, Random House (1938)

6. *LADDERS OF FIRE*, Anaïs Nin, Dutton (1946)

7. *THE PRICE OF SALT*, Claire Morgan, Coward-McCann (1952)

8. *ODD GIRL OUT*, Ann Bannon, Fawcett (1957)

9. *HOUSE OF INCEST*, Anaïs Nin, Centaur (1958)

10. *JOURNEY TO A WOMAN*, Ann Bannon, Fawcett (1960)

11. *THE DESERT OF THE HEART*, Jane Rule, Seeker & Warburg (1964)

12. *LA BÂTARDE*, Violette Leduc, Farrar, Straus & Giroux (1965)

13. *MRS. STEVENS HEARS THE MERMAIDS SINGING*, May Sarton, Norton (1965)

14. *APPLESAUCE*, June Arnold, McGraw-Hill (1966)

15. *PATIENCE AND SARAH*, Isabel Miller, McGraw-Hill (1971)

16. *LES GUÉRILLÈRES*, Monique Wittig, Viking (1971)

17. *CONFESSIONS OF CHERUBINO*, Bertha Harris, Harcourt, Brace & World (1971)

18. *THE FEMALE MAN*, Joanna Russ, Bantam (1975)

19. *MOURNING THE DEATH OF MAGIC*, Blanche McCrary Boyd, Macmillan (1977)

20. *RUBYFRUIT JUNGLE*, Rita Mae Brown, Bantam (1977)

16 Lesbians Who Wrote Autobiographies

1. CHARLOTTE CHARKE, *A Narrative of the Life of Mrs. Charlotte Charke (Youngest Daughter of Colley Cibber, Esq.)*, 1775. In the past, the designation "Mrs." meant a mature, though not necessarily married, woman.

2. CHARLOTTE CUSHMAN, *Memories of Her Life*, 1881.

3. GEORGE SAND, *Story of My Life*, 1854.

4. ANNA COGSWELL WOOD, *The Story of A Friendship: A Memoir*, 1901. This autobiography is about her 33-year Boston marriage with Irene Leache.

5. MARY MACLANE, *The Story of Mary MacLane, By Herself*, 1902. This work contains the story of her love for her teacher, Fanny Corbin. However, fifteen years later in *I, Mary MacLane: A Diary of Human Days*, MacLane repudiates her passion for Fanny, calling it "twisted." Contemporary lesbian scholar Lillian Faderman attributes the change in attitude to the rise in the 1920s of Freud and other sexologists who cast romantic friendships in a deviant light.

6. MARGARET ANDERSON, *My Thirty Years' War*, 1930. Anderson also wrote *The Fiery Fountain*, 1951, and *The Strange Necessity*, 1969.

7. MABEL DODGE LUHAN, *Intimate Memoirs*, Vol. 1, 1932. *Intimate Memoirs* tells about the intimate relationships Luhan had with other women during her youth.

8. ALICE JAMES, *The Diary of Alice James*, 1934.

9. DR. ALAN L. HART (ALBERTA LUCILLE HART), *The Undaunted*, 1936.

10. VIDA SCUDDER, *On Journey*, 1937.

11. I.A.R. WYLIE, *My Life with George*, 1940. George was Dr. Josephine Baker.

12. DOROTHY STRACHEY BUSSY, *Olivia*, 1949, under the pseudonym "Olivia."

13. NANCY SPAIN, *Why I Am Not A Millionaire*, 1955. Spain was a mystery writer who set one of her books in an all-girls school named Radcliff Hall. Her autobiography details her long-time relationship with Joan Werner Laurie.

14. SYLVIA BEACH, *Shakespeare and Company*, 1959.

15. ALICE B. TOKLAS, *What is Remembered*, 1963, and *Staying On Alone*, 1973.

16. ADRIENNE MONNIER, *The Very Rich Hours of Adrienne Monnier*, 1976.

"It was love itself I wanted to describe ... I write at a steady three hours a day with Isabelle's river tresses in my mouth, in my throat..."
—Violette Leduc, lesbian novelist and author
of *Thérèse and Isabelle*

1 Lesbian
Who Wrote a Kiss-and-Tell Book—
and the 7 Women She Blabbed About

In her 1960 autobiography, *Here Lies the Heart*, Mercedes de Acosta claimed to have been intimate with the following women — among others:

1. ISADORA DUNCAN, pioneer of modern dance

2. MARLENE DIETRICH, movie star

3. ALICE B. TOKLAS, Gertrude's honey

4. MARIE LAURENCIN, French painter

5. EVA LE GALLIENNE, Broadway actress

6. MALVINA HOFFMAN, American sculptor

7. GRETA GARBO, one of the screen's greatest beauties

6 Early Black
Lesbian and Bisexual Writers

As with many other early lesbians, it is hard to know if black women — many of whom were in even worse economic plights than their white counterparts — were actually lesbian. Our best clues come from letters and autobiographies, but few of the women specifically said they were gay.

1. ANGELINA WELD GRIMKÉ, 1880-1958

A black niece of the famous white abolitionist Angelina Emily Grimké, Angelina Weld Grimké is best known for her poems *Rosabel* and *Autumn.*

Like most of the women in this list, she was married, but gay scholars researching her life are beginning to ask more about the relationships with the women in her life. Her unpublished works reveal many love poems to women.

2. LORRAINE HANSBERRY, 1930-1965

The first black to have a play produced on Broadway, Hansberry was awarded the New York Drama Critics' Circle Award for *A Raisin in the Sun* during the 1958-59 theater season. At age twenty-nine, she was the youngest American ever to receive the coveted prize. Hansberry also wrote *The Sign in Sidney Brustein's Window, Les Blancs, What Use Are Flowers?* and *The Drinking Gourd.*

Hansberry, too, was married, and her "lesbianism" is indicated by early anonymous letters sent to *The Ladder,* one of the first lesbian magazines in the U.S. When she was twenty-six, Hansberry wrote to the magazine to defend lesbianism as a political choice.

Unfortunately for history and for literature, Hansberry died at an early age. Had she lived in the 1980s, she might have come out of the closet.

3. FRANCES E.W. HARPER, 1825-1911

A Unitarian and an abolitionist, Harper was also known for her poetry and her novels. She was first published in 1845, and her *Eventide* appeared in 1854, but she is best known for *Iola Leroy: Or Shadows Uplifted*, an 1892 novel. In addition to her novels, she wrote poetry and short stories under the pen name of Effie Afton.

Like many activists of the day, she spoke on the lyceum circuit — the college lecture circuit in today's terms.

4. ZORA NEALE HURSTON, 1891-1960

Hurston was a part of the Harlem Renaissance. Her best known work is the 1937 novel *Their Eyes Were Watching God*. She also wrote an autobiography, *Dust Track on a Road*, which describes her relationship with "Big Sweet," a black woman of immense physical courage and outrageous language.

Although not openly gay, Hurston wore men's clothes — and seemed to play the part — during much of her life. Her eccentric ways got her into trouble in 1948 when she was accused of molesting a boy. The white *and* black media hounded her, destroying her career and nearly her life.

5. GEORGIA DOUGLASS JOHNSON

A Southern poet, Johnson had four volumes of poetry published during her lifetime; they have recently been reprinted. *The Heart of a Woman and Other Poems* was published in 1918; *An Autumn Love Cycle* in 1928.

Although her letters reveal love relationships with women, she is best known in the heterosexual world for her affair with W.E.B. DuBois.

6. ALICE MOORE DUNBAR-NELSON, 1875-1935

Although overshadowed by her husband, the nationally recognized black poet Paul Laurence Dunbar, Nelson was a poet in her own right. An activist who worked as a journalist, she was much in demand as an orator. Her letters reveal at least two intimate relationships with women.

9 Novels with Black Lesbian Themes or Characters *

1. *HOME TO HARLEM*, Claude McKay (1928)
   Two scenes in this novel are set in black lesbian bars and show a glimpse of Harlem in the period following World War I.

2. *YOUNG MAN WITH A HORN*, Dorothy Baker (1938)
   Josephine Jordan, a black singer, has a relationship with Amy North, a wealthy woman.

3. *THE WASTELAND*, Jo Sinclair (1946)
   This novel's lesbian circle includes a black woman whose character, while not well developed, shows the oppression of black women.

4. *THE BIG MONEY*, John Dos Passos (1960)
   Dos Passos has an episode that also includes a portrait of Harlem in the 1920s.

5. *LOVING HER*, Ann Allen Shockley (1974)
   Shockley's novel was among the first to explore interracial relationships between lesbians in all their complexity.

6. *STRANGE BROTHERS*, Blair Niles (1975)
   Like its Parisian counterpart, Harlem in the 1920s has been a major source of inspiration for black lesbian culture; this book draws on that source.

7. *RUBY*, Rosa Guy (1976)
   A transplanted West Indian girl finds friendship with a school chum.

8. *IN HER DAY*, Rita Mae Brown (1976)
   In this novel, Brown includes a long-time friendship between Adele, a wealthy black lesbian, and Carole, a white working-class lesbian.

9. *ED DEAN IS QUEER*, N.A. Diaman (1978)
   A black activist lesbian is elected mayor of San Francisco in this novel by a gay male author.

*This list was compiled from the book *Black Lesbians*, by J. R. Roberts.

22 Lesbian Poets

1. SAPPHO, fl. about 610-580 B.C., Greece
The most famous poet of the ancient Greek world, Sappho was referred to by Plato as the "Tenth Muse." She was one of the first poets to write the personal type of poem we know today. Few of her poems survived but those that do are clear, concise, and beautiful. Her name has come to denote lesbianism.

2. LOUISE LABÉ, c. 1524-1566, France
Labé was called "La Belle Cordière"; her sonnets are considered some of the best love poems in French literature. Over 1,500 poems were dedicated to a woman, Clémence de Bourges.

3. ANNA SEWARD, 1747-1809, England
Seward wrote most of her poems to Honora Scheyd although she had romantic attachments to Elizabeth Cornwallis, Penelope Weston, and others.

4. WU TSAO, b. about 1780, China
Wu Tsao was so popular in her day that her poems were set to music and sung across China. She wrote erotic poems to her women lovers and even to courtesans. Her work is included in the anthology *The Orchid Boat.*

5. EMILY DICKINSON, 1830-1886, U.S.
Recent scholars such as Patterson, Faderman, and Woodul have argued that Dickinson's "seemingly curious" life makes sense if seen from a lesbian perspective that includes the many women who were close to her, such as Sue Gilbert and Kate Scott Turner.

Like a contemporary multi-media artist, Dickinson wrote her poems on small scraps of paper which she sewed into booklets. Only two of her many poems were published during her lifetime and she died without knowing how renowned her work would become.

6. ELIZA COOK, d. 1889, England

This little-known poet wrote love poems to lesbian actress Charlotte Cushman.

7. RENÉE VIVIEN, 1877-1909, England

Born Pauline Tarn in London, Vivien spent most of her short life in Paris. She was part of Natalie Barney's circle, and one of the first lesbian writers since Sappho to celebrate lesbian love openly and proudly.

8. ANGELINA WELD GRIMKÉ, 1880-1958, U.S.

Grimké was influential in the Harlem Renaissance of the 1920s with such poems as *Under the Days* and *El Beso* (The Kiss). A political activist, she also wrote a 1916 protest drama entitled *Rachel.*

9. AMY LOWELL, 1874-1925, U.S.

Poems in *Sword Blades and Poppy Seed, Pictures of the Floating World, What's O'Clock* and *Ballads for Sale* are about her long-time companion, actress Ada Russell, who quit the stage to live with Lowell at her mansion. Lowell had a love of the theater and is also believed to have written passionate poems to famed actress Eleanora Duse.

Lowell — who smoked cigars, slept during the day, and wrote poetry at night — often disguised her work by using the masculine gender.

10. SARA TEASDALE, 1884-1993, U.S.

The most popular poet of her day, Teasdale may have found peace and companionship late in life with Margaret Conklin, one of her students.

11. CHARLOTTE MEW, 1869-1928, England

Many of Mew's poems appeared in magazines of the day and one volume, *The Farmer's Bride,* was published in 1916. She committed suicide in 1928. *I So Liked Spring, The Quiet House,* and *Saturday Market* have lesbian overtones.

12. AKIKO YOSANO, b. 1878, Japan

Yosano's poem *Tangled Hair*, about Yamakawa Tomiko, started a rage for sex-tousled hair that lasted for many months in Japan.

13. H.D. (HILDA DOOLITTLE), 1886-1961, England

An Imagist, H.D. is considered one of the finest modern poets. Although she married poet Richard Aldington and had an affair with Ezra Pound, she lived the latter part of her life with the novelist Bryher.

14. MARIANNE MOORE, 1887-1972, U.S.

A graduate of Bryn Mawr, Moore was friends with Pound and Williams of the Imagist school of poetry. She also likened herself to the fable writer La Fontaine, whom she translated. Many of her works of poetry reflect her identification with nature and animals. *O to be a Dragon* and *The Arctic Ox* show this love.

15. EDNA ST. VINCENT MILLAY, b. 1892-1950, U.S.

Millay became the first woman to receive a Pulitzer Prize, with *The Harp Weaver and Other Poems* in 1923. *The Lamp and the Bell* was probably modeled on Charlotte Babcock, an early love of Millay's. Millay called herself "Vincent."

16. DAME EDITH SITWELL, 1877-1964, England

Awarded the title Dame in 1954, Sitwell wrote poems, biographies, and an autobiography. In the 1920s, some of her poems were set to music by William Walton. The result, *Façade*, has become a classic.

17. MURIEL RUKEYSER, 1913-1980, U.S.

Rukeyser's work is marked by a social conscience that also led to two arrests — for associating with blacks in the 1930s South and for anti-war activities in the 1960s. She also visited Hanoi during the Vietnam War.

18. ELIZABETH BISHOP, 1911-1979, U.S.

Bishop was the first woman and first American to win the prestigious Neustadt International Prize for poetry in 1976. Unfortunately, her family recently refused to let her poems be used in the book, *Gay and Lesbian Poetry of Our Time*, despite Bishop's involvement with women.

19. MAY SARTON, b. 1912, Belgium

Sarton has lived most of her life in America. She writes prolifically and has published many volumes of poetry, fiction, and non-fiction.

20. ADRIENNE RICH, b. 1929, U.S.

Her first volume of poetry, *A Change of the World*, was published in the Yale Series of Younger Poets. Although married, Rich's involvement with feminism has been the inspiration for many of her poems, including *Of Woman Born*.

Since the 1970s, Rich has become a strong spokeswoman for lesbian-feminism. *Twenty-One Love Poems* and *Dream of a Common Language* grew out of this new self.

21. ELSA GIDLOW, b. 1898, U.S.

Gidlow's volumes of poetry have such wonderful titles as *Sapphic Song*.

22. OLGA BROUMAS, b. 1949, U.S.

Her first book of poems, *Beginning With O*, was chosen for the Yale Younger Poets series in 1977. Broumas has since published *Caritas* and *Soie Sauvage*.

7 Lesbians Whose Poems Appear in the Norton Anthology of Poetry, First Edition

1. ELIZABETH BISHOP

2. EMILY DICKINSON

3. H.D. (HILDA DOOLITTLE)

4. EDNA ST. VINCENT MILLAY

5. MARIANNE MOORE

6. ADRIENNE RICH

7. DAME EDITH SITWELL

6 Lesbian Photographers of the Past *

1. EMMA JANE GAY, b. 1830, U.S.

Gay founded a girls' school in 1856. She later became a photographer in order to travel with the ethnologist, Alice Fletcher, a Native-American rights advocate who was studying the Nez Percé tribe of Idaho. The two women eventually settled together in Washington, D.C.

2. FRANCES BENJAMIN JOHNSTON, b. 1864, U.S.

Considered one of America's finest photojournalists, Johnston photographed coal miners and sailors as well as such notables of the day as Susan B. Anthony and Helen Hay Whitney, the lesbian poet.

3. ALICE AUSTEN, b. 1866, U.S.

Austen photographed many lesbians of the day; some of her work can be seen in the book, *The Revolt of American Women*. She and Gertrude Tate were lovers and lifelong friends.

4. BERENICE ABBOTT, b. 1898, U.S.

Abbott studied with Man Ray in Paris and had her own portrait studio there, where she photographed many lesbians such as Janet Flanner, Solita Solano, and Princess Eugene Murat as well as Gide, Cocteau, and other literati of the period.

5. SARAH HOLCOMB, b. 1846, U.S.

6. VISCOUNTESS CLEMENTIA HAWARDEN, b. 1822, England

Viscountess Hawarden was one of the earliest woman members of the Royal Photographic Society, London.

---

*This list was compiled from Judith Schwarz's introduction to *Eye to Eye: Portraits of Lesbians*.

9 Lesbian Artists

1. ROSA BONHEUR, 1822-1899, France

Famed for her animal and landscape paintings, Bonheur said she would rather paint bulls than men. She dressed in men's clothing and was eventually given legal permission to do so. She lived with Nathalie Micas for forty years. The love of her later life was Anna Klumpke.

2. ANNA KLUMPKE, nineteenth century, U.S.

An American, Klumpke settled in France and studied with Bonheur. Klumpke also wrote a biography of Bonheur.

3. EMMA STEBBINS, b. 1815, U.S.

Part of actress Charlotte Cushman's circle of lesbians in Europe, Stebbins was a sculptor and lover of Cushman.

4. MARY EDMONIA LEWIS, 1843-1909, Black–Native American, U.S.

Lewis spent much of her life in Rome where she was a great success, despite her youth and race. She is best known for her paintings of Native Americans and for being part of the artistic set of Charlotte Cushman.

5. EMMA CROW, fl. 1830, U.S.

A sculptor, Crow was also involved with Cushman's "Jolly Female Bachelors."

6. HARRIET HOSMER, b. 1830, U.S.

One of the most successful sculptors of the day, Hosmer exhibited in Italy, England, and the U.S., where her statue of Queen Isabella was commissioned by the city of San Francisco.

7. MARY ANN WILLSON, fl. 1820, U.S.

Having had little training, Willson painted in what would now be called a "primitive" style.

8. MARIE LAURENCIN, 1883-1956, France

Laurencin was a friend of Gertrude Stein, and her work during her early involvement with the cubists is detailed in *The Autobiography of Alice B. Toklas*. A bisexual, Laurencin was married and her most publicized affair was with Apollinaire, although she also had relationships with women.

9. ROMAINE BROOKS, 1874-1970, U.S.

Born in the U.S., Brooks lived most of her life in Paris and was famous for her portraits of celebrities of the day. She had shows all over Europe and was awarded the Cross of the Legion of Honor. She only began to be recognized in her native land when the Smithsonian organized an exhibit of her work in 1971, years after her death.

"I would ask her
(1) How did you get rid of the hatchet?
(2) Did you commit the murders in the nude to avoid bloodstains?
(3) If not, where did you hide the bloody dress?
(4) What was Nance O'Neill like in bed? and
(5) What are you doing tonight?"

—Florence King, lesbian novelist and author of
Confessions of a Failed Southern Lady,
on Lizzie Borden, a lesbian she'd like to meet

11 Famous Standards
Seen Through Lesbian Eyes

Much debate surrounds the question of whether a lesbian or gay sensibility exists. Whether or not it does, art made by and for heterosexuals with little thought of homosexuality looks very different if seen from a lesbian perspective.

1. THE VENUS OF WILLENDORF

Small statues from the Paleolithic era of 20,000 to 30,000 years ago, of which this is the best-known example, are found throughout eastern Europe, France, the Ukraine, and Siberia. Made from ivory, stone, or baked clay, these earth-mother figures are four to five inches tall with ample breasts, belly, and buttocks. There are no distinct facial features.

The lack of individual facial features has led historians and archeologists into endless controversy about the meaning and function of these figurines. Some scholars say that their significance must have been sexual; others argue that there is no sexual component at all. Still others say they are fertility charms; the opposite school holds that they carry no fertility symbolism whatsoever. Some scholars say they were early religious icons while others say they have no religious significance at all.

To the lesbian eye, they are both religious and sexual fertility symbols. They come from an era when the evocation of female fertility — unfettered by the knowledge of the male role in procreation — reigned supreme and was considered the central magic of the universe.

2. MINOAN SNAKE GODDESS

This second-century B.C. statue shows the bare-breasted Goddess in full regalia. Carved of ivory, she wears a crown and has gold bracelets on her upper arms, while in her hands she holds two hissing snakes at bay with her magical power.

3. GABRIELLE D'ESTRÉES ET UNE DE SES SŒURS, Anonymous

This painting with a very coy title shows Gabrielle and one of her sisters in a titillating scene. In the front, one naked woman fondles the other's breast while a third woman sits in a back room busying herself with needlework. Curiously enough, one of the naked women is holding an engagement ring — as if she's about to throw it away or just took it off her finger to give to her lover.

4. *SLEEP*, Gustave Courbet

If this famous painting weren't entitled *Sleep*, the position of the two women — with legs entwined and one woman's head nearing the other's breast — would undoubtedly have kept the work from being exhibited. It's perfectly obvious that sleep is the last thing on this couple's mind.

Of all the standard pieces listed here, this 1866 painting by Courbet is the one in which the lesbian overtones were most likely intended. A sophisticated artist, Courbet was undoubtedly familiar with the full spectrum of sexuality, but played the art game with aplomb by painting an outrageous scene, then giving it a coy title to make it respectable.

5. *DIE JUNGFRAU*, Gustav Klimt

Entitled *The Young Maids* or *The Virgins*, Klimt's 1913 painting has a number of young women encircling each other, heads touching under a quilt-like bed of flowers and swirls. The central figure has her eyes shut — as if she were savoring the embrace of the woman lying near her. That woman's head can just be seen peeking out from the quilt — as if she had just come up for air.

6. *LES DAMES DU BOIS DE BOULOGNE*, Anonymous

This 1925 French photograph shows two naked ladies, arms entwined at the waist and suitably bobbed in the "liberated" look of the day, stepping into the back seat of a roadster. One appears to be inviting the other into the car. Or perhaps they have just agreed that in the absence of anything better, the back seat of a roadster will have to do.

7. *WHITE FLOWER*, Georgia O'Keeffe

Lesbian and feminist "cunt" art took off in the 1970s but the first such pieces were O'Keeffe's flower paintings done as early as the 1920s. Any number of these gems show the exuberance of Mother Nature at her most explicitly erotic and female.

8. *LIBERTY, LEADING THE PEOPLE*, Delacroix

In this painting, three Amazons lead the peasants to depose Louis XVI during the French Revolution of 1789 with their call for Liberty, Equality, and Fraternity. Apparently the U.S. Post Office found the original to be a bit much. Its stamp version has the bare-breasted leader missing one essential element — the nipples.

9. *LIBERTAD*, Siqueiros

A twentieth-century revolutionary painting, this rendition of Liberty shows a modern, maddened Amazon breaking the chains of oppression. The artist, Siqueiros, is of the few painters to ever personalize the popular figure of Liberty by giving her an expression of rage.

10. *REVOLUCIÓN*, Francisco Eppens

This modern painting by another of Mexico's revolutionary artists shows a fighting Amazon with wings of sword blades flying through the air toward her enemies. She wields a knife and bayonet — and wears a round of ammunition between her breasts.

11. MONA LISA, Leonardo da Vinci

Ever since the Mona Lisa was painted, her enigmatic expression has tortured critics. She isn't the usual shy flower that most heterosexual artists paint; she certainly doesn't have the "come-hither" look most men expect of their women. And her self-satisfied smile has them completely baffled. Frustrated critics keep asking "What can it possibly mean?"

Any lesbian could tell them the answer in a second. This bold, proud woman will look any man in the eye because she's their equal. She's not some demure sex object, because she doesn't need them. In other words, she doesn't dance the heterosexual dance. Nor, apparently, did Leonardo. He was gay himself and most likely gave the world one of its first portraits of an independent lesbian.

7 Lesbian Musicians, Composers, and Opera Divas

1. FELICITA VON VESTVALI, b. 1824, Polish contralto
   A superstar of her day, this world-famous diva was known as "Vestvali the Magnificent" and was offered a subsidy by the Mexican government; she resided in Mexico until the Revolution. She was also known for her stage portrayals of Romeo and Hamlet.

2. LILI BOULANGER, b. 1893, French composer
   The first woman to be awarded the Prix de Rome, Boulanger wrote many compositions before death cut her down in her mid-twenties.

3. EMMA CALVÉ, b. about 1863, French opera soprano
   Calvé was part of Natalie Barney's Paris circle.

4. RENATA BORGATTI, early twentieth-century pianist
   Borgatti was also part of Barney's famous group of society lesbians.

5. DAME ETHEL SMYTH, b. 1858, English composer
   Part of the First Wave of women's suffrage, Smyth composed *March of the Women* in 1911, the same year she was imprisoned for civil disobedience. In her later years, she was given the honor of being made a Dame of the British Empire in recognition of her musical talent. An autobiography, *Impressions that Remained*, is part of her literary output.

6. WANDA LANDOWSKA, 1879-1959, Polish harpsichordist
   Landowska almost singlehandedly revived the harpsichord, which had fallen into disfavor as a concert instrument. A prime trooper, she recorded her acclaimed rendition of Bach's *Well-Tempered Clavier* at age seventy.

7. HENRIËTTE BOSMANS, b. 1895, Netherlands composer and pianist
   Bosmans lived with cellist Frieda Belinfante for seven years.

10 Famous Black American Lesbian Singers and Entertainers

1. BESSIE SMITH, 1894-1937

Bessie Smith almost singlehandedly put black blues on the map, combining songs of the rural South with an instinct for theater that made blues accessible to people all over the country. Her brand of theatrical acumen contributed to the Harlem Renaissance. Some of her music survives on records and she can be seen in two films, one of which is *St. Louis Blues.*

A biography by Chris Albertson revealed that Smith had many women lovers. One — Boula Lee — was upfront about her lesbianism even though she was married to Bill Woods, Smith's musical director. Although Smith, too, was married, her touring company had many such bisexual and lesbian women, and Smith's affairs with women were a continual source of conflict with her husband, Jack Gee.

2. MA RAINEY, 1886-1939

Born in Columbus, Georgia, Rainey was known as a "woman-lovin' woman" in her day, and there is speculation that the term originated with her. In lesbian circles her best-known song was *Prove It on Me Blues.*

3. BESSIE JACKSON

A blues singer from the 1920s and 1930s, Jackson, too, was fairly open about her sexuality, singing about it in the lyrics to *B.D. Woman's Blues.*

4. GLADYS BENTLEY, 1907-1960

A singer and pianist known for her risqué lyrics to popular songs, Bentley wore men's clothes and caused a scandal when, dressed as a man, she tried to marry a woman in Atlantic City. However, she eventually had hormone treatments, became a heterosexual, and renounced her past.

5. LIBBY HOLMAN

An actress and entertainer of the 1920s and 1930s, Holman sometimes dressed in men's clothes and reportedly had an affair with famed American chanteuse Josephine Baker.

6. JOSEPHINE BAKER, 1906-1975

Although married a number of times, Baker is often included in the lesbian pantheon because of her loving relationships with other women. However, she is most remembered today in her adopted country, France, for her torch songs. By the time of her death in 1975, she was considered one of France's national treasures and had been awarded the Croix de Guerre for her work in the French Resistance during World War II.

In her later years, she adopted a dozen children of all nationalities and called her family the "Rainbow Tribe."

7. TINY DAVIS

Davis played trumpet for the International Sweethearts of Rhythm, an interracial, all-woman band that toured the U.S. from the late 1930s through World War II. When it disbanded, she formed her own band, Tiny Davis and Her Hell-Divers.

8. RUBY LUCAS

Lucas, who was Tiny Davis's lover, also played piano, bass, and drums in Davis's band. Lesbian filmmakers Greta Schiller and Andrea Weiss have made a documentary about the two.

9. MOMS MABLEY, 1897-1975

A black comedian who became nationally known in the 1960s, Mabley was renowned for her earthy wit.

10. ALBERTA HUNTER, 1895-1984

A blues singer from the early part of the century, Hunter made a comeback in the 1980s. Her work is freely available on record and can be heard in Alan Rudolph's little-known but fascinating female-revenge film *Remember My Name.*

13 Fave-Rave Lesbian Songs:
A Queer Dozen *

1. *LEAPING (LESBIANS)*, by Sue Fink and Joclyn Grippo

2. *AMAZON ABC*, by Alix Dobkin

3. *IMAGINE MY SURPRISE*, by Holly Near

4. *SWEET WOMAN*, by Cris Williamson

5. *ODE TO A GYM TEACHER*, by Meg Christian

6. *SURPRISE (I'M A LESBIAN)*, by Paula Walowitz

7. *ROSALIE*, by Bonnie Hayes, performed by Teresa Trull

8. *WOMANLY WAY*, by Linda Tillery

9. *OLDER WOMEN*, by Lynn Lavner

10. *MADEMOISELLE*, by Lucie Blue Tremblay

11. *SISTERSHIP*, by Faith Nolan

12. *WOMAN-LOVING WOMEN*, by Teresa Trull

13. *THE LESBIAN POWER AUTHORITY*, by Alix Dobkin

*This list was compiled by Toni Armstrong, publisher of *Hot Wire: Journal of Women's Music and Culture* and a columnist for Chicago's *Outlines* newspaper.

10 Lesbian Patrons of the Arts

1. JULIE RÉCAMIER, 1777-1849, France

Married to a rich, older man at an early age, Récamier's Paris salon attracted the literati of her day. She inspired passion among both men and women although her relationships with men were said to be platonic in an age known for its decadence. She was a faithful romantic friend of the writer and literary patron, Madame de Staël, however.

2. MADAME DE STAËL, 1776-1817, France

Forced into an arranged marriage, de Staël had many affairs during her life but her relationship with Récamier lasted through them all. Their correspondence shows the intense passion that two women could have toward one another even while married. De Staël's salons were famous whether she was entertaining in Paris or exiled in Switzerland.

3. CHARLOTTE CUSHMAN, 1816-1876, U.S.

A superstar actress, Cushman helped many other actresses and artists as well as expatriate Americans during the years she resided in London and Rome.

4. NATALIE BARNEY, 1876-1972, U.S.

Born of an upper-crust family, Barney spent most of her life in Paris, where she was known as "L'Amazone" for her upfront lesbianism. Despite this, her weekly salons attracted every artist who passed through Paris. The lesbian guests often tended to congregate in separate rooms during these soirées.

Barney set up a foundation to help struggling writers such as T.S. Eliot, Paul Valéry, and Renée Vivien. In 1949, she endowed a Renée Vivien prize for women poets.

5. SYLVIA BEACH, 1887-1962, U.S.

Beach, too, lived in Paris, where she ran the Shakespeare and Company bookstore, which carried books in English for expatriate Americans (Gertrude Stein was a regular patron). Beach is known for fighting to publish James Joyce's classic, *Ulysses*, when the other houses were frightened of accusations of obscenity.

6. MARGARET ANDERSON, b. about 1873, France

Anderson founded *The Little Review*, which helped create the literary renaissance of Paris in the 1920s, with her lover Jane Heap. Together they launched the careers of many writers, including H.D.'s love, Bryher.

7. JANE HEAP, d. 1964, London

Heap and her lifelong lover Margaret Anderson held salons in their Paris flat, which was as well known for the bed that hung from the ceiling as for the artists and writers who congregated there.

8. & 9. CHERYL CRAWFORD and MARJO JONES, twentieth century, U.S.

These two women produced some of gay playwright Tennessee Williams's first plays.

10. ELSA MAXWELL, b. 1883, U.S.

Maxwell was one of the first public relations professionals. In addition to promoting her artists and writers, she was hired by Monaco to promote Monte Carlo and by Italy to pitch the Lido. A friend of Cole Porter's, she led the rich on fabulous, pre-jetset jaunts. She also saw that many of her starving artist friends met the people who could help them with their careers.

"I'd rather be a free spirit and paddle my own canoe."
—Louisa May Alcott, spinster and author of a
nineteenth-century novel about romantic friends.

5 Works with Natalie Barney
as a Character

Perhaps more than any other lesbian, Natalie Barney inspired fictional portrayal; she provided the basis for a character in at least five novels and books of poetry.

1. *IDYLLE SAPHIQUE*, Liane de Pougy

2. *L'ANGE ET LES PERVERS*, Lucie Delarue-Mardrus

3. *LADIES ALMANACK*, Djuna Barnes

4. *THE WELL OF LONELINESS*, Radclyffe Hall

5. *LETTRES À L'AMAZONE*, Rémy de Gourmont

9 Non-Fiction Books
Every Lesbian Should Own *

1. *WOMAN PLUS WOMAN*, Dolores Klaich, 1974

2. *SISTERHOOD IS POWERFUL*, Robin Morgan, 1969

3. *LESBIAN/WOMAN*, Del Martin and Phyllis Lyon, 1972

4. *SEX VARIANT WOMEN IN LITERATURE*, Jeannette Howard Foster, 1956

5. *SAPPHO WAS A RIGHT-ON WOMAN*, Sydney Abbott and Barbara Love, 1972

6. *OUR RIGHT TO LOVE*, Ginny Vida, 1978

7. *LESBIAN IMAGES*, Jane Rule, 1975

8. *LOVE BETWEEN WOMEN*, Charlotte Wolff, 1972

9. *FROM THE CLOSETS TO THE COURTS*, Ruth Simpson, 1976

*This list was compiled by Barbara Grier, lesbian activist, publisher, and founder of The Naiad Press.

12 Lesbian Actresses

1. CHARLOTTE CHARKE, fl. 1775, England
As was common at the time, Charke played male roles on stage and wore men's clothes offstage as well. She lived with a number of different women.

2. CHARLOTTE CUSHMAN, 1816-1876, U.S.
Cushman, whose acting talent was celebrated throughout Europe and America, developed a circle of lesbian friends called the "Jolly Female Bachelors." She and Rosalie Kemble Sully, daughter of the American artist Thomas Sully, were lovers.

3. FANNY KEMBLE, 1809-1893, England
Kemble was a friend of Charlotte Cushman in her early days but then married an American plantation owner. Always a radical, she became an abolitionist due to this experience.

4. ADAH ISAACS MENKEN, 1835-1868, France
Menken's poems about lesbian love made her scandal of the day. Her friendship with another outrageous eccentric, flamboyant bisexual author George Sand, didn't help either.

5. MARGUÉRITE MORÉNO, early twentieth century, France
Moréno was a friend of Colette during Colette's lesbian, music hall days — which are politely referred to as her "bohemian" period.

6. EMILIE MARIE BOUCHARD, d. 1939, France
Another friend of Colette from her music hall days, Bouchard went by the stage name Mlle. Polaire. She was also known for the minuscule size of her waist during the "Belle Époque," an era of notoriously tightened waists and even tighter corsets.

7. ADA RUSSELL, early twentieth century, U.S.
Also known as Ada Dwyer, Russell gave up her stage career to live with poet Amy Lowell at "Sevenals," the Lowell family estate.

8. EVA LE GALLIENNE, b. 1899, England
Le Gallienne was a Broadway stage actress who started the Civic Repertory Theater.

9. KATHARINE CORNELL, 1893-1974, Germany
Cornell was so popular that she was called "The First Lady of the American Theater."

10. BLYTH DALY, early twentieth century, U.S.
Daly spent so much time at the Algonquin Hotel that she dubbed Eva Le Gallienne, Estelle Wynwood, Tallulah Bankhead, and herself "the four horsemen of the Algonquin."

11. NANCE O'NEILL, early twentieth century, U.S.
O'Neill is best remembered today for being the lover of accused hatchet-murderer Lizzie Borden.

12. MARIA SCHNEIDER, b. 1952, Belgium
Schneider checked herself into a mental hospital to be near her lover, heiress Patty Townsend. She plays the lead in two films: Antonioni's *The Passenger* and Bertolucci's *Last Tango in Paris.*

> "I think of lesbians as the real women, women undistorted by needing to stay within the usual boundaries for women. In Boulder, years ago, during the statewide conference for women, the lesbians were in one corner: barefoot, wild-haired, t-shirted and wonderful. Everyone else looked so confined."
> —Joanna Russ, lesbian science fiction author

12 Broadway Plays
with Lesbian Themes or Characters *

1. *A FLORIDA ENCHANTMENT*, 1896
In this play, a sex change leads to an onstage kiss between two women. Ushers had ice water ready for the audience during intermission in case anyone felt faint.

2. *THE GOD OF VENGEANCE*, 1907
The proprietor of a house of prostitution tries to ensure that his daughter isn't corrupted by the men visiting his home — but she becomes involved with a female prostitute. This play came to Broadway after being staged in Poland, Austria, Italy, Sweden, Norway, Holland, and Russia.

3. *THE CAPTIVE*, 1926
A French diplomat's daughter is seduced into a long-term lesbian relationship. The play premiered in Paris.

4. *WINTER BOUND*, 1929
The script included a dyke who swears like a man and totes a whip.

5. *GIRLS IN UNIFORM*, 1932
This was the English adaptation of Christa Winsloe's play *Mädchen in Uniform*. The play only lasted a dozen performances, and the movie opened four months later.

6. *THE CHILDREN'S HOUR*, 1934
Lillian Hellman's drama about two schoolteachers accused of lesbianism played seven hundred times in New York and over a hundred on tour but was banned in Boston and London. It was revived in 1945 and 1952.

7. *WISE TOMORROW*, 1937
A young actress leaves her fiancé for an older woman. This play

flopped on Broadway but was a tremendous success in London.

8. *LOVE OF WOMEN,* 1937
For some unexplained reason, a man comes between two women who have made a brilliant career of writing plays. The drama closed after five days on Broadway but was another smash in London.

9. *TRIO,* 1945
This play about the breakup of a lesbian relationship was closed after two months by the Commissioner of Licenses. But there was such a storm of protest that it was the last time a play was closed because of a lesbian or gay man on stage.

10. *NO EXIT,* 1946
This typically heavy philosophical drama by Jean-Paul Sartre is about a lesbian who steals a man's wife, then drives her to suicide. It lasted a month in New York after playing two years in Paris.

11. *SOMETHING UNSPOKEN,* 1953
Tennessee Williams's one-acter is about the closeted relationship of a Southern lady and her "private secretary."

12. *THE KILLING OF SISTER GEORGE,* 1966
In this play-within-a-play, a successful career woman steals a butch's baby doll. It was later made into a movie.

*This list was compiled from the book *We Can Always Call Them Bulgarians,* by Kaier Curtin.

24 Early Movies
with Lesbian Characters or Actresses *

1. *SALOMÉ*, Alla Nazimova, 1923
   Lesbian Nazimova produced and starred in this movie version of the Oscar Wilde play.

2. *MARE NOSTRUM*, Rex Ingram, 1926
   This movie portrays a spy who claims to be a lesbian.

3. *PANDORA'S BOX*, G.W. Pabst, 1929
   Pandora's Box was the first movie to show a lesbian couple on the screen. It starred Louise Brooks as "Lulu" and Alice Roberts as "Countess Geschwitz," her lesbian admirer.

4. *MÄDCHEN IN UNIFORM*, Leontine Sagan, 1931
   This tragic film, based on Christa Winsloe's play, had two versions. In one, the young heroine jumps to her death; in the other, she is rescued at the last moment by her classmates.

5. *THE CHILDREN'S HOUR*, William Wyler, 1936 and 1961
   Two schoolmistresses are accused of lesbianism by a student. Although the play brought fame to Lillian Hellman, Hollywood censors forced her to change the sex of one of the teachers in the filmscript. Twenty-five years later Wyler remade the film, restoring the integrity of the original.

6. *CLUB DES FEMMES*, Jacques Duval, 1938
   Some of the dialogue from the lesbian subplot was cut by U.S. government censors.

7. *DANGEROUSLY THEY LIVE*, Robert Florey, 1942
   This movie included a Nazi lesbian, Connie Gilchrist.

8. *THE SINNERS*, Julien Duvivier, 1949
   Nadine Basile portrayed a lesbian in prison in this film.

9. *YOUNG MAN WITH A HORN*, Michael Curtiz, 1950
   Here, Lauren Bacall plays a lesbian who takes a young woman artist to Paris with her. The film is based on the Dorothy Baker

novel of the same name, though the lesbianism in the novel was more intense.

10. *PIT OF LONELINESS*, 1954
Originally a French melodrama titled *Olivia*, this film was renamed in order to capitalize on the fame of Radclyffe Hall's *Well of Loneliness*. It was set in a girls' boarding school, and included the obligatory tragic ending. This version, however, was scripted by Colette.

11. *THE GODDESS*, 1958
Lesbian tendencies surface when nurse Elizabeth Wilson takes charge of disintegrating film goddess Kim Stanley.

12. *LOSS OF INNOCENCE*, Lewis Gilbert, 1961
Also called *The Greengage Summer*, this film includes two lesbian lovers.

13. *A WALK ON THE WILD SIDE*, Edward Dmytryk, 1962
Barbara Stanwyck plays a lesbian madame in a New Orleans brothel in this adaptation of the Nelson Algren novel.

14. *THE L-SHAPED ROOM*, Bryan Forbes, 1962
This "kitchen-sink" drama includes a busybody spinster whose one great love was a woman.

15. *THE BALCONY*, Joseph Strick, 1963
In this adaptation of Jean Genet's play, Shelley Winters falls for Lee Grant.

16. *FROM RUSSIA WITH LOVE*, 1963
The only redeeming feature of this deplorable James Bond movie is Lotte Lenya as Col. Rosa Krebs, a lesbian spy. Other Bond films which also have male fantasies of lesbians who get theirs in the end are *Goldfinger* and *Live and Let Die*.

17. *SYLVIA*, Gordon Douglas, 1965
Viveca Lindfors plays a lesbian librarian, one of the many lesbian roles this fine actress has played during her wide-ranging career.

18. *PERSONA*, Ingmar Bergman, 1966
This typically slow Bergman film depicts Liv Ullman as a lesbian.

19. *THE GROUP*, Sidney Lumet, 1966

Candice Bergen, as a lesbian, gives a jerk husband whose wife has committed suicide his just desserts in this adaptation of Mary McCarthy's novel.

20. *TONY ROME*, 1967

A lesbian alcoholic appears with her lover — a strip-tease artist.

21. *THE FOX*, Mark Rydell, 1968

Adapted from the D.H. Lawrence novel, this film shows a lesbian couple that is destroyed when a fox in the form of Keir Dullea gets into the henhouse. In this typical heterosexual male fantasy, when one woman is killed, the other blithely goes off with the man — her attachment to the woman forgotten.

22. *LES BICHES*, Claude Chabrol, 1968

This male fantasy includes Stéphane Audran as a lesbian seductress.

23. *THE KILLING OF SISTER GEORGE*, Robert Aldrich, 1968

This film was one of the first that did not have a heterosexual cure at the end, even though it still has a tragic ending. Beryl Reid plays a swaggering, alcoholic soap opera star, Susannah York her baby-femme girl friend, and Carol Browne the predator who steals York. The movie was partially filmed at The Gateways Club, a lesbian bar in London, allegedly with "real-life lesbian extras."

24. *FRÄULEIN DOKTOR*, Alberto Lattuada, 1969

Lesbian spy Capucine puts the make on Suzy Kendall.

*This list was compiled from the book *The Celluloid Closet,* by Vito Russo.

"Lois Lane is a lesbian."

—Jill Johnston, lesbian author

14 Cult Films with Lesbian Characters

1. *DRACULA'S DAUGHTER*, 1936
   Countess Alesca appears as a lesbian vampire.

2. *CHILDREN OF LONELINESS*, 1939
   Not shown until 1953, this campy documentary about a lesbian and gay man has a narrative overlay by a psychiatrist who warns of the evils of homosexuality à la *Reefer Madness*.

3. *GIRLS IN PRISON*, 1956
   Prison lesbians.

4. *BLOOD AND ROSES*, 1960
   Roger Vadim film about lesbian vampires.

5. *THE HAUNTING*, 1963
   Claire Bloom blames ghosts for her advances toward Julie Harris.

6. *WHO KILLED TEDDY BEAR?* 1965
   Elaine Stritch is a lesbian victim.

7. *CHELSEA GIRLS*, 1966
   The underground Andy Warhol movie with lesbians and gay men has a maximum of talk and a minimum of action.

8. *BELLE DU JOUR*, 1967
   A surrealist film by Buñuel with S&M overtones, *Belle du Jour* has Genevieve Page as a lesbian madame.

9. *THE LEGEND OF LYLA CLARE*, 1968
   A drug addict falls for Kim Novak.

10. *VAMPIRES*, 1974
    Two hitchhiking lesbian vampires kill men.

11. *THE WILD PARTY*, 1975

This James Ivory movie includes a Hollywood version of lesbians. Ivory is the other half of the gay Merchant-Ivory team that produced *Maurice*.

12. *THE HUNGER*, 1983

Catherine Deneuve, Susan Sarandon, and David Bowie are vampires.

13. *REFORM-SCHOOL GIRLS*, 1986

Punk-rock star Wendy O. Williams is a leather-clad dyke.

14. *BECAUSE THE DAWN*, 1988

This modern lesbian vampire movie was made by and for lesbians.

12 On-Screen Kisses and Slow Dances

1. *MANSLAUGHTER*, 1922
Cecil B. De Mille includes two lesbians kissing in the orgy scene.

2. *MOROCCO*, 1930
A small peck from Marlene Dietrich appears in an otherwise heterosexual film.

3. *QUEEN CHRISTINA*, 1933
Greta Garbo, as Queen Christina of Sweden, kisses Elizabeth Young as Countess Ebba Sparre, the great love of Christina's life. Garbo allegedly told actress Katharine Cornell that she would also like to play Dorian Gray in Oscar Wilde's *The Picture of Dorian Gray*.

4. *A WOMAN'S FACE*, 1941
This film has a scene with two women dancing.

5. *OPEN CITY*, 1945
Rossellini's famed film includes a lesbian seduction scene with Italian actresses Giovanna Galletti and Maria Michi.

6. *RACHEL, RACHEL*, 1968
A lonely schoolteacher springs a surprise kiss on Joanne Woodward but promises never to try it again.

7. *THERESE AND ISABELLA*, 1968
The lesbian scene in this movie, with a title from the well-known lesbian novel, verges on soft porn.

8. *THE CONFORMIST*, 1970
Bertolucci's film about fascism features a sensual dance scene with Dominique Sanda and Stefania Sandrelli.

9. *ONCE IS NOT ENOUGH*, 1975

Melina Mercouri and Alexis Smith are lesbians in this adaptation of Jacqueline Susann's novel of the same name.

10. *PERSONAL BEST*, 1982

Mariel Hemingway and Patrice Donnelly star as Olympic athletes and ill-fated lovers.

11. *LIANNA*, 1983

Except for the corny lesbian bar scene, John Sayles's low-budget independent realistically depicts a woman who leaves her husband for a lesbian, only to find that the woman has a girlfriend elsewhere.

12. *DESERT HEARTS*, 1986

Donna Deitch's movie includes a graphic but well-done love scene between Helen Shaver and Patricia Charbonneau. Though independently financed, Deitch's Hollywood movie is probably the first film produced and directed by a lesbian that is seen from a lesbian point of view and shows a lesbian relationship with a happy ending.

58 Actresses Who Have Played Lesbian or Bisexual Women in Movies

1. JANE ALEXANDER, *A Question of Love*
2. JUNE ALLYSON, *They Only Kill Their Masters*
3. ELIZABETH ASHLEY, *Windows*
4. STÉPHANE AUDRAN, *Les Biches*
5. LAUREN BACALL, *Young Man With a Horn*
6. TONI BASIL, *Five Easy Pieces*
7. PAMELA BELLWOOD, *The War Widow*
8. CANDICE BERGEN, *The Group; The Adventurers*
9. CLAIRE BLOOM, *The Haunting*
10. TOMI-LEE BRADLEY, *A Perfect Couple*
11. DYAN CANNON, *Doctors' Wives*
12. CAPUCINE, *Fräulein Doktor*
13. GERALDINE CHAPLIN, *A Wedding*
14. PATRICIA CHARBONNEAU, *Desert Hearts*
15. CHER, *Silkwood*
16. CATHERINE DENEUVE, *The Hunger*
17. SANDY DENNIS, *The Fox*
18. PATRICE DONNELLY, *Personal Best*
19. PATTY DUKE, *By Design*
20. TOVAH FELDSHUH, *The Women's Room*
21. MEG FOSTER, *A Different Story*
22. GRETA GARBO, *Queen Christina*
23. WHOOPI GOLDBERG, *The Color Purple*
24. LEE GRANT, *The Balcony*
25. MARIETTE HARTLEY, *My Two Loves*
26. MARIEL HEMINGWAY, *Personal Best*
27. AUDREY HEPBURN, *The Children's Hour*
28. ANNE HEYWOOD, *The Fox*

29. LINDA HUNT, *Waiting for the Moon*

30. LOTTE LENYA, *From Russia With Love*

31. VIVECA LINDFORS, *Sylvia; Puzzle of a Downfall Child*

32. SHIRLEY MacLAINE, *The Children's Hour*

33. MARIANGELA MELATO, *To Forget Venice*

34. MELINA MERCOURI, *Once Is Not Enough*

35. BETTE MIDLER, *The Rose*

36. SYLVIA MILES, *The Sentinel*

37. GENEVIEVE PAGE, *Belle du Jour*

38. ESTELLE PARSONS, *Rachel, Rachel*

39. VALERIE PERRINE, *Lenny*

40. DONNA PESCOW, *All My Children*

41. LYNN REDGRAVE, *My Two Loves*

42. BERYL REID, *The Killing of Sister George*

43. RACHEL ROBERTS, *Doctors' Wives*

44. GENA ROWLANDS, *A Question of Love*

45. DOMINIQUE SANDA, *The Conformist*

46. SUSAN SARANDON, *The Hunger*

47. HELEN SHAVER, *Desert Hearts*

48. ALEXIS SMITH, *Once Is Not Enough*

49. BARBARA STANWYCK, *A Walk on the Wild Side*

50. STELLA STEVENS, *Cleopatra Jones and the Casino of Gold*

51. MERYL STREEP, *Manhattan*

52. ELIZABETH TAYLOR, *X, Y and Zee*

53. INGRID THULIN, *The Silence*

54. CATHY TYSON, *Mona Lisa*

55. LIV ULLMAN, *Persona*

56. WENDY O. WILLIAMS, *Reform School Girls*

57. SHELLEY WINTERS, *The Balcony; Cleopatra Jones; S.O.B.*

58. SUSANNAH YORK, *The Killing of Sister George; X, Y and Zee*

6 Bisexual Dancers and Courtesans of the Gay Nineties *

1. LOIE FULLER, 1862-1928

Fuller was born in America but made her name in Paris. She inspired the swirling Art Nouveau style of the day with the long lighted silks she used in her dances. She herself was inspired by the natural elements and based her work on them. *Rainbow*, *Butterfly*, and *Clouds* were but a few of the indoor atmosphere pieces she created before actually moving the performances outside to capture the full effect of light and sound.

2. ISADORA DUNCAN, 1877-1927

Also born in the U.S., Duncan met Fuller early in her career. By the time of her tragic death, Duncan's style of dancing — which is credited with founding modern dance — had taken her through triumphant tours in Europe, South America, the U.S., and Russia.

3. LOUISE WEBER, "La Goulue"

A well-known Paris courtesan at a time when café society and courtesans were at their height, Weber can be seen in many of Toulouse-Lautrec's sketches, including "LaGoulue."

4. LIANE DE POUGY, b. 1870

Another famed courtesan of "Belle Époque" Paris, de Pougy had an affair with Natalie Barney and wrote about it in the 1901 novel, *Idylle saphique*. The character "Flossie" is based on Barney.

5. EMILIENNE D'ALENÇON

A friend of Pougy's, d'Alençon is mentioned in her *My Blue Notebooks*.

6. MATA HARI, 1876-1917

The daughter of a wealthy Dutch merchant, Gertrud Margarete Zelle MacLeod changed her name to "Mata Hari" after leaving her husband. Her exotic beauty, semi-nude dancing, and bohemian lifestyle won her instant fame. She was a member of the Natalie Barney circle at its most roaring.

Mata Hari was accused and convicted of being a German spy during World War I and was executed by a firing squad in 1917. There is still controversy as to her guilt.

*This list is based on information taken from *Women Who Love Women*, by Tee Corinne.

"Only three times in my life have I met a genius and each time a bell within me rang."
—Alice B. Toklas of her lifelong partner,
novelist Gertrude Stein

7 Lesbians Behind the Scenes

1. DOROTHY ARZNER
Arzner was an early Hollywood director. Her films include the 1937 movie, *The Bride Wore Red* with Joan Crawford and *The Wild Party* in 1929.

2. ELIZABETH MARBURY
Marbury was an early twentieth-century theater manager who later became a politician. She was also openly involved with another woman, Elsie de Wolfe.

3. JAN OXENBERG
A contemporary American independent director, Oxenberg has made lesbian comedies such as *Home Movie*.

4. BARBARA HAMMER
A contemporary American independent, Hammer has made such underground lesbian films as *Superdyke, Dyketactics*, and *No No Nooky T.V.*

5. MONIKA TRUET
Truet, a contemporary German director, has made *Virgin Machine, Seduction: The Cruel Woman*, and *Bondage*.

6. DONNA DEITCH
Deitch is a contemporary Hollywood director who was known for her early documentaries — such as the feminist film *Woman to Woman* — before producing the highly-acclaimed lesbian drama, *Desert Hearts*. Deitch also directed the made-for-TV movie, *Women of Brewster Place*.

7. MIDI ONODERA
A contemporary Canadian independent filmmaker, this Asian lesbian has made such films as *The Displaced View*, and *Ten Cents a Dance (Parallax)*.

8 Lesbians on Television

Since the introduction of cable TV, numerous television shows have been made by, for, and about lesbians. But before this recent development, lesbians were either invisible or portrayed as losers and weirdos. Today, lesbians are appearing increasingly often on network television via documentaries about such themes as lesbians drummed out of the military (*Sally Jessy Raphael*) and lesbian couples who use artificial insemination to have children (*20/20*).

1. *POLICE WOMAN*
In 1974, this show featured three lesbians who kill the residents of a retirement home. Despite vociferous protests, it was aired. (ABC)

2. *A QUESTION OF LOVE*
Originally a made-for-TV movie about a lesbian fighting for the custody of her children, this 1978 drama is now on video. The story was based on an actual court case. (ABC)

3. *THE WAR WIDOW*
This 1976 little-known, made-for-TV movie by Harvey Perr featured a lesbian love affair.

4. *MY TWO LOVES*
Rita Mae Brown wrote the script for this made-for-TV movie featuring a tortured Lynn Redgrave who had to choose between a man and a woman.

5. *GOLDEN GIRLS*
In one episode, an older woman shocked the three man-hunting regulars by revealing her lesbianism. (NBC)

6. *HEARTBEAT*
Aaron Spelling's beleaguered medical drama was one of the first TV series to feature a lesbian in a positive light. Soon after its

introduction, however, a protest campaign was launched by right-wing fundamentalists. Until the show was finally cancelled, allegedly for low ratings, Marilyn McGrath — played by Gail Strickland — was seen with her lover, Patty, once a week. (ABC)

7. *TWO IN TWENTY*

A soap opera which features seven lesbians, this Boston cable program by Laurel Chiten and Cheryl Qamar is now being shown in movie theaters. It includes lesbian parodies of commercials.

8. GAY CABLE NETWORK (GCN)

Formed in New York in 1982, GCN produces a number of gay and lesbian shows: *TV: Pride and Progress*, a political program; *The Right Stuff*, gay entertainment; and *Be My Guest*, a gay and lesbian game show. It also airs a news program in magazine format, *The 10% Show*, which is being aired in Atlanta, Nashville, New Orleans, San Francisco, Los Angeles, Chicago, and Cincinnati.

9 Lesbian Videos

Videotape recorders have been in wide use for a decade. In that time, independent video production companies have created videos of every imaginable variety for every imaginable market — including lesbians.

1. *LESBIONAGE*, available from Pop Video

This lesbian mystery featuring two lesbian private eyes was shot on location in Washington, D.C., in such hot spots as Lammas, the local feminist bookstore. It includes cameo appearances by lesbians such as black poet Jewelle Gomez.

2. *IMAGES*, Tri-Image

"Will she or won't she?" is the question this video poses for a woman who is half of a couple but still drawn to a known homewrecker.

3. *REFLECTIONS*, Tri-Image

Two women who meet through a classified ad struggle through their own racism while trying to create a relationship.

4. *FAMILY VALUES*, Hands-On Productions

Although not produced or directed by lesbians, this documentary deserves the highest recognition because it depicts the many lesbians who are a crucial part of the fight against AIDS. The many fascinating women portrayed range from Emily Rosenburg of PAWS (Pets Are Wonderful Support) to Sky Renfro (International Ms. Leather Contest).

5. *FANTASY DANCER*, Lavender Blue Productions

This video combines fantasy and erotica with a sense of humor. A woman imagines herself joining an erotic dancer to make love on the stage; once that's done, she leaves her boyfriend for the woman.

6. *HAY FEVER*, Tigress Productions

An erotic, melodramatic comedy set in the Old West, this video features two sisters who find adventure after adventure as they travel to a round-up for the reading of their mother's will.

7. *EROTIC IN NATURE*, Tigress Productions

Released in 1985, this was among the first erotic videos made by lesbians. Like most erotic videos, it makes up for in sex what it lacks in dialogue.

8. *BURLEZK LIVE*, Fatale Video

This half-hour video includes computer animation and safe-sex information for lesbians.

9. *LESBIAN DESIRE*, Bean Blossom Productions

Here is more lesbian erotica from the group that brought us *Lesbian Dildo Fever* and *Lesbian Dildo Bondage*. Enough said!

5 Lesbian Journalists

1. LAURA DE FORCE GORDON, b. 1838, U.S.

Journalist, activist, and lawyer, Gordon fought her first political battle when she tried to enroll in law school. She and a friend, Clara Foltz, had to fight for admission to Hastings College of Law; their case went all the way to the California Supreme Court.

Gordon began her newspaper career in 1873. She became an editor for papers in Stockton, Oakland, and Sacramento before she turned to public speaking on behalf of women's suffrage.

Her book, *The Great Geysers of California*, was unearthed in a San Francisco time capsule in 1979. On the flyleaf, Gordon had written, "If this little book should see the light of day after 100 years' entombment, I should like the readers to know that the author was a lover of her own sex and devoted the best years of her life in striving for the political equality ... of women."

2. MARGARET FULLER, 1810-1850, U.S.

An educator and transcendentalist as well as a journalist, Fuller worked on the *New York Tribune* both in the U.S. and abroad. She was best known in her day for her book *Woman in the Nineteenth Century*, the American equivalent of Wollstonecraft's *Vindication of the Rights of Women*.

During her short life, Fuller had romantic friendships with English suffragettes Harriet Martineau, Caroline Sturgis, and Elizabeth Peabody. She also translated into English the passionate correspondence between German romantic friends Karoline Von Günderode and Bettine von Arnim. Fuller married the Marchese d'Ossoli when she became pregnant and died in a shipwreck off the coast of New York soon thereafter.

3. LORENA HICKOK, b. 1893, U.S.

Hickok was covering the White House for the Associated Press when President Franklin D. Roosevelt asked her to investigate the effects of the Great Depression in the U.S. Her moving reports of poverty, sent to FDR from across the country, encouraged the president's implementation of the New Deal.

Hickok later became involved with First Lady Eleanor Roosevelt, whose marriage to FDR had long since turned into a comfortable companionship. Hickok and Eleanor exchanged sapphire rings as well as passionate correspondence for many years.

4. DOROTHY THOMPSON, 1893-1961, U.S.

Thompson was one of the first women journalists to cover a foreign country for a major newspaper, but she was kicked out of Nazi Germany in 1933 for her condemnation of Hitler. Thompson was married three times, once to muckraking novelist Sinclair Lewis, who probably wrote the novel *Ann Vickers* with Thompson in mind. Thompson also lived with Christa Winsloe, author of *Mädchen in Uniform*, for a time.

Although Thompson loved different women during her life, she despaired of her bisexuality.

5. JANET FLANNER, 1892-1978, U.S.

Flanner is most famous for her work as "Genêt" in the *New Yorker* magazine. She was part of Natalie Barney's Paris circle and was one of the lesbians satirized by Djuna Barnes in *The Ladies Almanack*. She was also friends with Gertrude Stein and Alice B. Toklas. In later life, Flannery helped organize a fund for Toklas to live on during the latter's poverty-stricken final years.

5 Contemporary
Syndicated Lesbian Columnists

An explosion in the gay and lesbian press since 1980 has allowed contemporary lesbian jounalists to syndicate their work and be published nationally.

1. CHRISTINE BURTON, *The Thought Connection*
   In addition to her column, Burton has founded an organization for older lesbians called *Golden Threads*.

2. AMPARO JIMENEZ, *Encuentro Latino*
   Jimenez, a recent immigrant to the U.S., reaches many Hispanic lesbians with her Spanish column and has helped organize the Latino community in Chicago.

3. LEE LYNCH, *The Amazon Trail*
   Lynch writes a personal view of life from a rural hideaway. A collection of her columns was published as a book under the same title.

4. LOUISE RAFKIN, *The Woman's Page*
   Rafkin is also the author of a book of short stories, *Unholy Alliances*.

5. YVONNE ZIPTER, *Reflections*
   Zipter's recent book, *Diamonds Are a Dyke's Best Friend*, isn't about the glittery gem but about something even better — softball diamonds.

10 Contemporary Lesbian Theorists

1. CHARLOTTE BUNCH

An early member of the feminist movement, Bunch helped edit *Quest: A Feminist Journal* and edited such books as *Lesbianism and the Woman's Movement* and *Women Remembered* with Nancy Myron. Her latest book is *Passionate Politics: Feminist Theory in Action.*

Bunch is currently the Director of the Douglass Center for Global Issues and Women's Leadership at Rutgers University.

2. SUSAN CAVIN

A founding editor of New York City's *Big Apple Dyke News*, Cavin has written extensively on feminism and lesbianism. Her book *Lesbian Origins* posits a unique view of the origins of society. She theorizes that all-women Amazon tribes evolved from the high-female/low-male ratio of primary kinship groups that are still seen today in primates, our nearest relatives. These Amazon tribes spanned the globe and preceded the heterosexual, patriarchal society of equal female-to-male kinship groups that we know today.

3. MARY DALY

A doctor of theology and philosophy, Daly has documented her journey from Catholicism to lesbian feminism in many books, including *Beyond God the Father; The Church and the Second Sex; Gyn/Ecology;* and *Pure Lust.*

Her 1978 article *Sparking: The Fire of Female Friendship* was one of the first to deal with female friendships and how the phenomenon relates to lesbianism.

4. ANDREA DWORKIN

Like Daly, Dworkin has been influential in connecting violence against women and the daily holocaust it brings with the treatment of Jews in Nazi Germany and other oppressed people. Her many books include *Woman Hating; Intercourse; Pornography;* and *Right-wing Women.*

5. JUDY GRAHN

Grahn was once best known for her poetry, but her meditations on language and symbols in *Another Mother Tongue* drew accolades as much for their personal, emotional style as for their impressive content.

6. SUSAN GRIFFIN

Griffin is another poet whose work became part of lesbian theory when she published *Woman and Nature*. The book is particularly striking in that it dispenses with the traditional essay form to incorporate short poetic prose pieces into the medium of discourse.

7. SARAH LUCIA HOAGLAND

Two of Hoagland's books of theory, *Lesbian Ethics* and *For Lesbians Only: A Separatist Anthology* (the latter edited with Julia Penelope), burst on the scene in 1988. As Hoagland herself admits, *Ethics* is not easy reading. But for anyone interested in the questions raised, it is well worth the extra mental effort that philosophy sometimes takes.

8. SONIA JOHNSON

Johnson became a "cause célèbre" when she was excommunicated by the Mormon church in 1979 for her stand on feminism. She has since written about this period of her life in the fascinating book *From Housewife to Heretic*.

A theorist who is especially conscious of the part religion plays in lesbian-feminist oppression, she is also the author of *Going Out of Our Minds* and *Wildfire*.

9. SUSAN McGREIVY

McGreivy, a civil rights lawyer who has worked for many years with the American Civil Liberties Union as well as the Lesbian and Gay Community Services Center, is known for what she has termed *The Lost Seed Rights*, a theory of patriarch oppression.

10. ARLENE RAVEN

An art critic and historian, Raven taught at the Feminist Studio Workshop and was instrumental in founding the Los Angeles Woman's Building in the mid-1970s. She has published essays in many lesbian and feminist journals over the years and recently edited *Feminist Art Criticism: An Anthology* with Cassandra L. Langer and Joanna Frueh.

10 Amazon Treatises

1. *SEXUAL POLITICS*, Kate Millett, 1971

2. *S.C.U.M. MANIFESTO*, Valerie Solanas, 1971

3. *MOTHERS AND AMAZONS*, Helen Diner, 1973

4. *LESBIAN NATION*, Jill Johnston, 1973

5. *WOMEN REMEMBERED*, Nancy Myron and Charlotte Bunch, 1974

6. *GYN/ECOLOGY*, Mary Daly, 1978

7. *ON STRIKE AGAINST GOD*, Joanna Russ, 1980

8. *POLITICAL LESBIANISM: THE CASE AGAINST HETEROSEXUALITY*, Leeds Revolutionary Feminist Group — Lal Covency, Tina Crockett, Al Garthwaite, Sheila Jeffreys, and Valerie Sinclair, 1981

9. *LESBIAN ORIGINS*, Susan Cavin, 1985

10. *THE DEMON LOVER: ON THE SEXUALITY OF TERRORISM*, Robin Morgan, 1989

Amazon Queens
and Other Exotics

11 Amazon Queens *

1. PENTHESILEIA, fl. 1200 B.C., Greece

According to Greek legend, Penthesileia was a fierce warrior queen who led Amazon troops in the Trojan war. She was killed in battle by Achilles.

2. BOADICEA, d. A.D. 62, Britain

British tradition holds that this queen of Norfolk led a Celtic-inspired revolt of some two hundred thousand people against the Roman conquerors when they tried to confiscate her land, money, and title after the death of her husband, the king. Her army sacked what were then Roman outposts of London, Colchester, and St. Albans, killing some seventy thousand retired soldier-settlers before Roman reinforcements could be brought in to stop her.

Today, there lies beneath the city of London a layer of scorched earth created by the fire that engulfed the city after Boadicea's attack. Scientists have estimated that the heat exceeded a thousand degrees.

Although Boadicea was eventually defeated and is thought to have committed suicide by poisoning, many lesbians feel her name (pronounced Boo-dee-ka) lives on in the word "bulldyke."

3. BRÜNNHILDE, c. 534-613, Austrasia

The Queen of the Visigoths, this warrior was nothing like the watered-down operatic version we know today. As queen, she was beholden to no one.

4. AETHELFLAED, d. 918, Saxony

The daughter of King Alfred, she co-ruled West Mercia with her husband Ethelred until his death in 911. After that, she came into her own. She roused the local armies to defeat the Vikings in East Anglia, and began an attack on what were then the Danish strongholds of Leicester and Derby. Prior to that expansion, she had gained control of Northumbria and Wales.

5. JUDITH, d. 977, Ethiopia

As Queen of the Falasha, Judith attacked the capital of

Ethiopia and captured the inhabitants. She is said to have ruled Ethiopia for forty years — until her death in 977.

6. ELEANOR OF AQUITANE, 1122-1202, France

Despite the stereotype we have today of medieval ladies sitting quietly in castles waiting for their husbands' return, most battened down the hatches, ran the village, and were strong leaders. Eleanor became Queen of France in her teens and led a troop of three hundred women warriors and nurses in the Crusades when she was in her twenties.

When her sons tried to take power, she sided with them against her husband, an act for which she was imprisoned. When released a decade later, she granted political amnesty to other prisoners. She was involved in politics till her death at the age, very advanced for those days, of eighty years.

7. TAMARA, d. 1212, Russia

The Queen of Georgia, this little lady was called "King Tamara" by her soldiers. A brilliant military strategist, she was also known for her tolerance and generosity.

8. ELIZABETH I, 1533-1603, England

A diplomat who ended an ongoing war with France and the Netherlands, Elizabeth I is best known for her defeat of the Spanish in 1588.

She was a virgin queen who refused offers of marriage all her life. Scholars are constantly trying to find the "man in her life." Some say she loved Robert Dudley or Robert Devereux, the Earl of Essex. But she had Devereux put to death after a rebellion against her, and Dudley, who was married, was more likely a friend from childhood. The most probable love of her life was power.

She struggled for many years before gaining the throne and British legend has it that soon thereafter a man questioned her right to rule because she was a mere woman. She ordered his right hand cut off and no one ever showed such impertinence again.

9. NZINGH, b. 1582, Africa

Queen of the Matamba tribe of southwest Africa, Nzingha realized the threat of the Portugese invaders from an early age.

During her brother's reign she helped negotiate a treaty with Portugal, but when she rose to the throne she rejected it. Instead, she allied her army with the Dutch to fight the invaders.

Although defeated, she was not vanquished. She retreated to the jungle and held the Portugese at bay during an eighteen-year guerrilla war. On her death at eighty-one, Angola finally fell into colonial hands.

While heroic, Nzingha's exploits were part of a long, rarely remembered African tradition of Amazon warriors that existed until modern times. During the nineteenth century, the King of Dahomey's army consisted of 2200 women warriors, out of a total of three thousand.

10. CATHERINE THE GREAT, Empress of Russia, 1729-1796

In 1762, Catherine engineered a coup d'état and took over the throne from her incompetent husband, the tsar — a wise move for personal and political reasons. During her long reign, she was regarded as a tolerant monarch who nevertheless expanded Russian territory, thereby increasing the population from twenty million to thirty-six million.

Catherine was a tomboy from an early age. Her sexual prowess was almost as well known as her military acumen. She believed sex was necessary for health, even in an age that thought sex for women was particularly debilitating. Voltaire called her the "Semiramis of the North" after the ninth-century B.C. queen of Babylon who was said to have put unsatisfactory lovers to death.

11. LAKSHMI BAI, b. about 1830, India

As the Rani of Jhansi, Lakshmi Bai roused fourteen thousand volunteers to fight the British when they tried to annex her kingdom following her husband's death. Although she fought valiantly, she is thought to have died from a wound received in hand-to-hand combat.

Her husband, Gangadhar Rao, was an actor who sometimes wore female dress offstage as well as on, and was reputedly gay.

*Material in this list was derived from *The Warrior Queens*, by Antonia Fraser.

4 Chinese Amazon Warriors *

1. HONG XUANJIAO
This woman led an all-female combat division during the Taiping Revolution of 1851-64, a peasant revolt. By the time the Taiping armies took Nanking there were forty women's armies, totaling some hundred thousand women.

Asia has a long history of women warriors, although the women who fought on North Vietnam's side during the war there were probably the first such warriors that Westerners had ever seen.

2. JIU JIN
Perhaps the best known of Chinese revolutionaries, Jui Jin also called herself Qinxiong, which means "compete with men." She wore men's clothes, wrote feminist poetry, and fought against all restraints placed on women.

A leader in Sun Yat-Sen's time, she wrote poems of freedom and was later tried for treason. She was born in 1879 and beheaded in 1907 by the Manchu government.

3. CH'IN LIANG-YU
Like many strong Chinese women, Ch'in Liang-yu was given the command of the army after her husband's death during the seventeenth century.

4. SHEN YUN-YIN
Another seventeenth-century Amazon, Shen Yun-yin took her father's place after he was killed by rebels. As the commander, she led the army to victory and brought her father's body back for burial.

---

*Material in this list was derived from *A Passion for Friends*, by Janice G. Raymond.

3 Amazon Acts from the Bible

1. LILITH, THE APOCRYPHA

According to the non-Canonized part of the Bible called the "Apocrypha," the first woman created was not Eve but Lilith, made at the same time and out of the same clay as Adam. She saw herself as equal rather than subservient to Adam and was driven out of the garden for her refusal to be a second-class citizen. As such, she was the first feminist.

2. JAEL, THE BOOK OF JUDGES

Jael assassinated the Canaanite general Sisera when he fled the Israelite army which, led by the prophetess Deborah and the military commander Barak, had just defeated his forces.

Jael offered Sisera hospitality when he tried to hide in her tent. She gave him milk and a bed. Then, when he went to sleep, she used a hammer to drive a tent pin through his temple.

We know of Jael through Deborah's poem celebrating the victory (Judges V), which is considered a triumph of lyric poetry and the oldest surviving piece of Hebrew literature.

3. JUDITH, THE APOCRYPHA

A pious young widow who prophesied that the Jews would be delivered from Nebuchadnezzar, Judith duped his general Holofernes into inviting her into his tent, got him drunk, and when he fell into a stupor, cut off his head.

The Baroque artist, Artemisia Gentileschi — one of the few early women artists whose work has survived the destruction of time — painted a startling rendition of this legendary act of women's history.

14 Amazon Cultures
of the Ancient World*

Much controversy revolves around the question of the Amazons — whether they were a historical fact or a mythological belief. Feminist theorists Helen Diner and Susan Cavin argue that Amazon culture based on homosexuality preceded heterosexual patriarchy as we know it today.

Using oral and written tradition, they posit these areas as past Amazon kingdoms.

1. LIBYA
During their rule, Libyan Amazons conquered northwestern Africa, Libya, Algeria, Egypt, Syria, and Lesbos. It was Libyan Amazons who, legend says, removed the right breast in order to fight more freely.

2. GORGONS (AFRICA)

3. GAGANS (NORTHWEST AFRICA)

4. PONTUS (ASIA MINOR)
Known as the Thermodontines, these Amazons were said to have had the capital of their kingdom on the southeast shore of the Black Sea in Hellenistic times.

5. ANATOLIA (ASIA MINOR)

6. LIBUSSA (CENTRAL EUROPE)

7. VALESKA (CENTRAL EUROPE)

8. RUS (EASTERN EUROPE)

9. THRACE (BALKAN PENINSULA)

10. INDIA

11. CENTRAL ASIA

12. ISLAND OF SAMOS

13. ISLAND OF PATMOS

14. SAMOTHRACE

In today's geographic terms, Amazons lived in Turkey, Georgian Soviet Socialist Republic (SSR), Armenian SSR, Azerbaijan SSR, Crimea, Bulgaria, Rumania, Libya, Algeria, Egypt, Syria, Lesbos, North Greece, India, China, and Mongolia.

*This information about Amazons comes from *Lesbian Origins*, by Susan Cavin.

> "A woman who loves a woman is forever young."
> —Anne Sexton, American poet

18 Sixteenth-
through Nineteenth-Century Areas
Said to Have Had Amazon Tribes

1. DAHOMEY

2. KATSINA

3. SIERRA LEONE

4. ANGOLA

5. ZANZIBAR

6. SOCOTRA

7. MALAWI

8. BRAZIL

9. GUIANA

10. PERU

11. COLOMBIA

12. NICARAGUA

13. WESTERN ANTILLES

14. CANADA'S PIEGAN LANDS

15. SINALOA

16. COLIMA

17. BAJA CALIFORNIA

18. ISLA DE MUJERES (ISLAND OF WOMEN), off Yucatan

8 Ancient Cities
Said to Be Founded by Amazons

1. AMASTRIS

2. CLETE

3. CYME

4. GRYNE

5. MAGNESIA

7. SINOPE

8. SMYRNA

8 Women-Identified Foremothers

Although not lesbian in the strictest sense, these women belong to the female separatist tradition. As founders of convents, they were known for their dedication to each other. They were responsible for the creation of the women-only sanctuaries which helped keep culture alive during the Dark Ages, following the collapse of the Roman Empire.

Centuries later, these women's communes had to fight for their very existence. The convents were frequently sacked by local lords who kidnapped and assaulted the women, then robbed them of their land.

1. AFRA, fourth century, Germany
Afra and three companion courtesans set up a convent when they converted to Christianity. They were eventually martyred for their beliefs and canonized. Today, Afra is the patron saint of "working girls."

2. HROTSVITA OF GANDERSHEIM, about 935-1000, Saxony
The abbess of a Benedictine nunnery, Hrotsvita was famous for her dramas; one of them is said to be the earliest version of the *Faust* story.

3. HILDA, 614-680, England
Abbess of the complex at Whitby, a Celtic monastery which fought the adoption of the Roman Easter celebration, Hilde was famous for her translation of Biblical stories from Latin to the language of the people.

4. EADGIFU, eleventh century, England
After a valiant battle, Eadgifu, the abbess of Leominster in Herefordshire, was captured by the Danish Earl of Swegen and kept prisoner for a year.

5. ST. CATHERINE OF SIENA, 1347-1380, Italy
A politician as well as a nun, Catherine is known for her extraordinary devotion to the poor. Less well known is that when

her mother suggested she try to look better to catch a husband, Catherine cut off her hair in defiance and joined a nunnery, having already vowed at an early age to remain a virgin.

6. FLORENCE BANNERMAN, sixteenth century, England

Bannerman, the abbess of Amesbury, fought the push to disband women's communes in sixteenth-century Britain.

7. TERESA OF ÁVILA, b. 1515, Spain

Teresa of Ávila is most famous for founding nearly twenty very strict convents during her life. Her name is also connected with Sappho, as she apparently loved a female cousin during her earlier years. Her biography, *The Eagle and the Dove*, by lesbian author Vita Sackville-West, was published in 1943.

8. JUANA INÉS DE LA CRUZ, 1652-1695, Mexico

A woman who said she joined a convent to escape the confines of marriage, Juana was an ardent feminist who wrote poetry and plays as well as a defense of women's education.

> "You are kissing away the venom of some angry hornet from my lips."
> —Sarah Edgarton's letter to her romantic friend, Luella Case, in the nineteenth century

4 Early Religious Orders Formed by Uppity Women

Prior to the witch burnings, many women were members of guilds where they earned their own living and thus could refuse to marry. Between 1354 and 1463, one-sixth to one-quarter of all taxpayers in Frankfurt, Germany, were single women.

1. BEGUINES, France

2. HEREFORD, Great Britain

3. GANDERSHEIM, Saxony (Germany)

4. QUEDLINBURG, Saxony

5,269 Uppity Women
Burned at the Stake

The European witch hunts during the fourteenth through seventeenth centuries reached a peak after the publication of the Revs. Kramer and Sprenger's *Malleus Maleficarum*. One of the most widely read books of the day, *Malleus Maleficarum* told how to ferret out a witch and how to torture her until she confessed.

The reign of terror that followed was so hysterical that nearly all the women in some towns were killed. During 1585, in the bishopric of Trier, two villages were left with only one woman each. In Toulouse, France, 340 witches were put to death in one day.

In Oppenau, over seven percent of the population were killed in less than one year, eighty-five percent of whom were women. In Como, 850 were burned at the stake in a year.

Estimates of the total women murdered run as high as three million during the three centuries that forced women into economic and heterosexual submission. Most of their names have been lost but the numbers remain.

340 — TOULOUSE, France, in 1 day

42 — OPPENAU, Germany, in 9 months

850 — COMO, Italy, in 1 year

765 — WÜRZBURG, Germany, in 1 year

63 — WIESENSTEIG, Germany, in 1 year

45 — OBERMARCHTAL, Germany, in 2 years

2,865 — VAUD, Switzerland, in 89 years

31 — LUCERNE, Switzerland, in 100 years

268 — ESSEX, England, in 120 years

11 Spinsters Accused of Witchcraft *

One of the most comprehensive studies of witchcraft accusations to date has been done on Essex, England by Alan Macfarlane.

Despite hundreds of accusations over a 100-year period, witchcraft accusations in Essex were a relatively mild affair compared to that of continental Europe. There were no accusations of conspiracy, sex with the devil, or midnight rituals until outside witch hunters came to town toward the end of the 120 years that comprised the period of accusations. All the same, nearly 300 witches were executed and twice that many accused from 1560 to 1680, the period for which extensive records are available.

Most of the people accused were old women. They were not poor enough to receive alms but they were poor enough to beg. More importantly, they were old enough to expect help from their neighbors. In fact, witchcraft accusations arose during a time of great economic change. As feudalism withered, the habit of voluntary mutual support among community members also deteriorated.

The gentry or rising yeoman class often led the accusations. These generally arose out of a refusal to help an old woman, who often cursed the refuser as a result. Since people still believed in magic, when something went wrong — from milk going sour or beer not brewing to animals and people becoming ill — witchcraft provided an answer to the question, "Why did this problem hit *me?*"

Single women and widows were the main targets of the accusations. If a married woman was accused, her husband was likely to be accused with her. Some were even accused by their own husbands. Many of the accusers — the "cunning folk" or "white witches" that townspeople sought for advice in pinpointing a witch — were men. Some were associated with the church, some were physicians and surgeons or members of the rising doctor class.

One characteristic of the women accused was that they were uppity. They would "curse" anyone who wouldn't give them help at a time when cursing was still a powerful emotional tool.

While no one today can know the sexual preference of any of the spinsters accused, a number of factors give us clues. Most of the women didn't have reputations as "bawds," i.e., they weren't known for sleeping with men. As such, we can assume that — like most lesbians — their sexuality could have been invisible to the heterosexual community.

Whatever their sexual preference, these women opted out of heterosexual patriarchy at its most basic level by remaining single. As a result, they were viewed with suspicion and treated as outsiders — with horrendous results. Many of the women were accused over and over again until they were finally found guilty and executed.

1. JOAN WATERHOWSE, 1566

Waterhowse was accused of witchcraft with Agnes Waterhouse and Elizabeth Fraunces. Joan Waterhowse confessed and was one of the few apparently acquitted after confession.

The disposition of Agnes Waterhouse's case is not known in this instance but she was accused again in 1584 and ended up dying of plague while in jail. Elizabeth Fraunces spent ten years fighting off witchcraft accusations and was jailed at least once.

2. ETHELREDA PILGRIM, 1576

Pilgrim was accused of bewitching Joan Masselyne but was found not guilty.

3. ELLEN SMYTHE, 1579

Smythe was accused of bewitching Susan Webbe, a four-year-old child. She was found guilty and executed. Her mother had also been executed for witchcraft.

4. ROSE PYE, 1580

Pye was accused of murdering Joanna Snow, a one-year-old child, by witchcraft. Since the townspeople were aware that children often died in infancy, Pye was acquitted.

5. MARGARET HOLBEYE, 1585

Holbeye was accused of bewitching Susan Pikas, another spinster, and sentenced to one year's imprisonment. She had already spent a year in prison for bewitching another woman.

6. KATHERINE REVE, 1585

Reve was accused of bewitching Helen Brownsmyth, found guilty, and imprisoned for one year. Prior to the 1585 accusation, Reve had been brought before the church court and made to do public penance for acts of witchcraft.

7. ELIZABETH SHYMELL, 1599

Shymell was accused of bewitching a cow and a pig but was found not guilty. She was brought to trial again that same year but the disposition of that case is not known.

8. PETRONELLA ABBOTT, 1600

Abbott was accused of bewitching Susan Dyxson but was acquitted.

9. ELIZABETH HUDSON, 1601

Hudson was first accused of bewitching William Charnoll and sentenced to be hanged, then was accused of bewitching Margaret Maynard. She confessed and was executed.

10. ELIZABETH HANKINSON, 1601

Hankinson was accused of bewitching Katherine Lawrence and John Ingate, both of whom died. She confessed, and was convicted and executed.

11. MARY HARTE, 1605

Harte was accused of bewitching seven pounds of meat because it putrefied; she was acquitted. A month later, she was accused of bewitching John Graye and Ursula Man. This time she was found guilty and was executed.

---

*This information is taken from *Witchcraft in Tudor and Stuart England*, by Alan Macfarlane.

9 Ways to Tell if a Woman Was a Witch

1. DISCOVERY OF A WITCH'S MARK.
   A witch mark was usually a spot on the face or protruding lumps on the body, but any odd mark, such as port-wine stains on the body, could be used against a woman. Witches were stripped naked and searched to find the marks.

2. ABNORMAL BODY HAIR FOR A FEMALE.

3. WARTS OR MOLES.

4. FAILURE TO SINK WHEN IMMERSED IN WATER.
   This practice was referred to as "ducking" or "swimming" someone.

5. HAVING "DEAD SPOTS."
   These areas made the witch unable to feel pain when poked or pricked with needles or other sharp instruments.

6. FAILURE TO BLEED.
   Witches were tested by being banged, scratched, or clawed.

7. RECOVERY OF THE WITCH'S PRESUMED VICTIM IF THE WITCH WAS THREATENED OR "DEFIED."

8. RECOVERY OF VICTIM IF THE WITCH HAD BEEN SCRATCHED OR PROPERTY SUCH AS HER HOME OR THATCH HUT WAS BURNT TO THE GROUND.

9. CONFESSION.
   In England, confessions were sought after a suspected witch had been kept awake, starved, beaten, and interrogated for days, or had been walked until the feet were blistered raw.
   In Europe, witches were also subjected to thumbscrews and spikes, the rack, and boots that crushed bones to make them "confess."

100,000 Chinese Marriage Resisters *

Calling themselves "tzu-shu nii" or "never to marry," Chinese women began refusing to marry in 1865 when the opening of silk factories in the Pearl River delta gave them economic independence.

They formed sister associations consisting of up to forty women who lived together in communes and swore sisterhood to the association. They also swore sisterhood to each other in pairs or threes. These sister societies were the women's main social and emotional bond.

To appease their families, the women performed their own marriage ceremony, which relieved the family of any obligation to the woman in her old age or death. As a result of this custom, they were also called "sou-hei" or "self-combers," because they then adopted a hair style that signified a married woman.

At its height, some hundred thousand woman belonged to this movement, but when the worldwide depression of the 1930s put an end to silk production, their numbers began to dwindle.

Because lesbianism was seen as a way to make the Chinese harem system workable, marriage resisters were tolerated at first. But once the Communist revolution succeeded, they were seen as a decadent product of Chinese feudalism.

At that point, the women began escaping to Hong Kong, Malaya, and Singapore. By 1955, they had set up 250 to 350 sisterhoods in Singapore alone. The women who had not fled China were treated ruthlessly during the Cultural Revolution. They were forced out of their associations and into re-education camps.

In 1986, some of the women could still be found in Hong Kong in Taoist vegetarian halls, or all-women old-age homes.

*The information in this list comes from *Sisters and Brothers, Lovers and Enemies: Marriage Resistance in Southern Kwangtung,* by Andrea Sakar.

11,000 and More Sworn Virgins

The custom of remaining a virgin was especially prevalent in fifth- through seventh-century Europe; the related custom of combining an oath of virginity with cross-dressing to avoid marriage is a tradition that has occurred often in the past two thousand years.

1. 11,000 VIRGINS OF ST. URSULA, about the fourth century

The legend of St. Ursula is based on a brief memorial in a Cologne basilica of the fourth or fifth century, which states that some holy virgins had been martyred on that spot. The figure of 11,000 is a later embellishment, but the number was probably large considering the ugly reputation of the invading Huns. A thousand years later, Columbus named the Virgin Islands in their honor.

2. ST. MARGARET, third century

St. Margaret took the male name "Pelagius" and became a monk after escaping an arranged marriage by jumping off a building the night before the wedding.

St. Margaret was particularly revered from the Middle Ages until the Renaissance. She was one of the saints who spoke to Jeanne d'Arc and gave her guidance.

3. ST. UNCUMBER

A Portugese princess, St. Uncumber refused to marry the King of Sicily when the opportunity for such a match arose. To escape, she swore virginity and was rewarded by being changed into a man. Proof of this miracle was the fact that she grew a beard.

St. Uncumber was a favorite saint of eleventh-century worshipers.

4. ANTOINETTE DE BOURIGNON, b. 1616

De Bourignon became a religious leader in Europe after dressing as a monk to flee an arranged marriage.

5. EASTERN EUROPEAN SWORN VIRGINS, nineteenth century

In the regions of Kosovo and Montenegro (modern Yugoslavia and Albania), the concept of sworn virgins existed from the 1800s until recent times.

A woman could avoid marriage and become a respected member of the community by taking on the mantle of a "sworn virgin." As such, she renounced traditional heterosexual marriage, vowed to remain chaste, and donned male clothing. In her new role, she was also allowed to carry weapons and to work in trades that were reserved for men.

For economic reasons, some sworn virgins were actually designated at birth in families with no sons. A young girl would sometimes choose to take on the role when a father or eldest brother died. She then became the head of the household and took on all the rights and responsibilities of the position.

Despite the vow of chastity, sworn virgins were allowed to take wives and often did.

7 Reasons for Remaining Single, from Ancient Greek and Hebrew Qualities of a Good Wife *

1. CHASTE

2. SOBER-MINDED

3. GOOD AT SPINNING, WEAVING, AND SEWING

4. BEING ECONOMICAL

5. CAN SING, DANCE, AND PLAY A MUSICAL INSTRUMENT

6. CAN STRING BEADS AND MAKE ARTIFICIAL FLOWERS

7. KNOWS MAGIC AND SORCERY

*This information comes from *Sex in History*, by Reay Tannahill.

15 Spinsters Who Need to Be Researched

Reading between the lines in the biography of a spinster often leads to a community of women, feminists, and romantic friends. There is no firm evidence that any of these women were lesbians, but more research on their lives might well turn up some surprises.

1. MAUDE ABBOTT, b. 1869
Abbott was a noted Canadian cardiologist and promoter of medical education.

2. JOSEPHA ABIERTAS, b. 1894
A Filipina lawyer and feminist, Abiertas was the first woman to graduate from law school in the Philippines.

3. MARIA AGNESI, 1718-1799
Agnesi, an Italian mathematician appointed to a professorship by Pope Benedict XIV, was known due to a confusion of language as the "Witch of Agnesi."

4. EMILY CARR, 1871-1945
A Canadian painter and writer, Carr felt like an "outsider" much of her life and spent many years living in rural areas surrounded by animals.

5. ANNA FREUD, 1895-1982
The daughter of the founder of psychoanalysis, Austrian Sigmund Freud, Anna was his secretary, companion, and pupil until striking out on her own to stress the developmental stages of child psychology. Some researchers believe Freud's famous case study of lesbianism is based on Anna.

6. SARAH MOORE GRIMKÉ, 1792-1873
An American feminist who also worked tirelessly for the abolitionist cause, Grimké never married but lived with her sister Angelina Emily and her sister's husband. The two women wrote

anti-slavery appeals together, lived, campaigned, and taught together until they retired in 1867.

7. ALICE HAMILTON, 1869-1970

Hamilton, an American doctor whose grandmother had been a friend of Susan B. Anthony, studied the effects of working conditions on health. Her research led to laws limiting the use of lead, nitrous fumes, and carbon disulphide in the workplace. She also worked with Jane Addams at Hull House for twenty-two years.

8. JESSIE KENNEY, 1879-1953

Jessie, the younger sister of English suffragette Annie Kenney, joined Christabel Pankhurst when Christabel escaped English treason charges by fleeing to Paris. There, they both spent time with Natalie Barney's crowd. Kenney was later the first woman to become an English radio officer.

9. ELLEN KEY, 1849-1926

Key was a Swedish feminist who wrote *Kvinnororeisen*, a study of the women's movement in her homeland.

10. ROSA MANUS, 1880-1942

A Dutch feminist, Manus was killed by the Nazis in the concentration camp of Auschwitz during World War II.

11. MARIA MITCHELL, 1818-1889

Mitchell spent her childhood helping her father with mathematical calculations used in sailing. She discovered a new comet while still in her twenties, which brought her instant fame. Mitchell was one of the first faculty members at the opening of Vassar Female College and later became the president of the American Association for the Advancement of Women.

12. OUIDA, 1839-1908

Ouida was the pseudonym of English novelist Marie Louise de la Ramée, who was known for her "flamboyant habits." That term is often a euphemism for lesbian ways or cross-dressing, but could also refer to bohemianism or affairs with men. Her novels include *Held in Bondage, Chandos,* and *Under Two Flags.* She died in Italy.

13. ELIZABETH PEABODY, 1804-1894

An American transcendentalist, Peabody published her brother Nathaniel Hawthorne's writing. In her later years, she became interested in early childhood education.

14. ELSA SCHIAPARELLI, 1896-1973

The Roman-born Schiaparelli is still famous for the tailored look of the couture clothes she designed. She never married and was often in the company of the lesbian artist Hannah "Gluck" Gluckstein.

15. MARY WHITNEY, b. 1847

An American mathematician who switched over to astronomy and became a student of Maria Mitchell's at Vassar College in 1865, Whitney later became Mitchell's assistant and eventually a professor in her own right. She worked tirelessly for women's education all of her life and on her deathbed said, "I hope when I get to heaven I shall not find the women playing second fiddle."

13 Uppity Women Who Were Called Lesbians — But Probably Weren't

The words for lesbian — "Sapphist," "tribadist," and the modern equivalents — have been used throughout the centuries to keep strong, outspoken women in their place. An 1838 pamphlet condemned Mary Wollstonecraft, Frances Wright, and Harriet Martineau for being "semi-women" and "mental hermaphrodites."

1. VALERIA MESSALINA, about A.D. 22-48, Rome

A Roman empress who was renowned for her sexual and political intrigue, Messalina was lumped together with Queen Elizabeth I, Jeanne d'Arc, and Catherine the Great when Dr. James Weir, Jr., in an 1895 anti-suffragette diatribe in *The American Naturalist* called them "viragints." The word "viragint" connoted lesbianism in late nineteenth-century Europe and America.

2. MME. DE MAINTENON, 1635-1719, France

The Princess Palatine accused a number of women of being Sapphists. These included Mme. de Monaco, Henriette d'Angleterre, and Mme. de Maintenon. The princess also called Queen Christina of Sweden a hermaphrodite.

3. LADY HARVEY, eighteenth century, England

In his memoirs about the amorous adventures of the English court during the eighteenth century, the count de Gramont named names — from the abbess of Chelles to the princess of the Asturias, the duchess of Mazarin, Mlle. Beverweert-Nassau, and Lady Harvey.

4. LADY MARY WORTLEY MONTAGU, 1689-1762, England

A learned bluestocking, Lady Mary was an outspoken advocate of women's education at a time when women were thought to be too frail for scholarly pursuits. Known in her day for the letters she wrote while traveling with her diplomat husband, Lady Mary also wrote satire and drama.

She was responsible for introducing smallpox inoculation to England, decades before Jenner invented vaccination. She had seen it in Turkey but the medical establishment of the day fought the concept tooth and nail. She convinced her friend, Queen Caroline, to have the queen's own children inoculated to prove it safe. The children lived, but one, the son and heir, nearly died. If he had, Lady Mary could have been arrested for treason as well as murder.

Lady Mary earned the name "Sappho" from Alexander Pope after she spurned his advances.

5. SOPHIE VOLAND, eighteenth century, France

Voland, Diderot's mistress, was called a lesbian by those who wanted her to stop interfering with the male domain of politics. She was said to be too heavily influenced by her sister, Mme. LeGendre.

6. MME. DE FLEURY, eighteenth century, France

In the novel *L'Espion anglois*, Mairobert caricatures a number of well-known and outspoken women of the day as lesbians. Mme. de Fleury was one; so were the actresses Raucourt and Souck.

7. LADY FRANCES BRUDENELL, eighteenth century, England

The Toast, by William King, satirized this erudite woman by giving her enough masculine cunning to outsmart the king. In the satire, her remarks were rewarded by Venus with a gift of male genitals, just the sort of added baggage a woman would always want.

8. MISS HOBART, eighteenth century, England

A maid of honor at the court of Charles II, Hobart was too bold for her sex. She was satirized in songs of the time as a hermaphrodite and was eventually ostracized by the nobles at court.

9. EMPRESS EUGÉNIE, 1826-1920, France

A sensational article by Petraccelli della Gattina in the *Cronaca Bizantina* magazine stated that Eugénie seduced young girls and encouraged lesbian practices among the women at Napoleon III's court. Eugénie was a powerful woman at the court and had thrown her weight against the French-Italian alliance which della Gattina supported.

10. SIRI VON ESSEN, early twentieth century, Sweden

In 1887 the playwright August Strindberg accused his wife, Siri von Essen, of lesbianism as well as debauchery with other men.

Sinclair Lewis — whose wife, Dorothy Thompson, left him for Christa Winsloe — did much the same thing, writing a negative novel about a lesbian after the breakup of his marriage. Conventional wisdom says to write about what you know...

11. VICTORIA WOODHULL, 1838-1927, U.S.

An ardent suffragist, Woodhull was called any number of epithets, including lesbian, for her strong support of equality for women and her resistance to the double standard of sexual morality.

She was also the first woman to run for president in the U.S. With her sister, Tennessee, Woodhull edited the *Woodhull and Claflin Weekly*. They also published the first English translation of Marx's *Communist Manifesto*.

Whatever might have been said about her private life, Woodhull married at least three times.

12. EMMELINE PANKHURST, 1858-1928, England

Pankhurst founded the Women's Social and Political Union. An outspoken activist, she was often imprisoned, and was called every name in the book — including lesbian — although she was married to a radical lawyer. She is often referred to as "Mrs. Pankhurst," to distinguish her from her daughters, Christabel, Sylvia, and Adela.

Christabel never married, and for a time was part of the lesbian feminist circle around the princess de Polignac.

13. GLORIA ALLRED, modern day, U.S.

This radical feminist lawyer was called a "slick butch lawyeress" in 1981 by conservative Republican State Senator John Schmidt. During a hearing on abortion, Allred presented him with a chastity belt. She later slapped Schmidt — who had called other feminists "Jewish dykes" — with a ten-million-dollar libel suit which she won.

17 Romantic Friends *

According to lesbian scholar Lillian Faderman, romantic friendships between women flourished in Europe and America during the seventeenth and eighteenth centuries and reached a peak in the nineteenth. Women pledged undying love to one another, were affectionate in public, and even lived together if they were independently wealthy or could earn a living at a time when women had very few economic options.

The love was seen as pure and spiritual, even surpassing that of heterosexual marriage, which was degraded by the flesh-ridden nature of sex. The world view of the time was so profoundly different from our own that these woman-to-woman emotional attachments were regarded as one of the highest attainments to which a woman could aspire.

Even married women had romantic friends. And at a time when heterosexual marriage was an economic necessity for most women, romantic friends were often a woman's only emotional outlet. Due to the prudery of the era, few suspected the women of engaging in sex even when they lived together, sharing the same house and bed.

The idyll came to a crashing halt when the sexologists of the early twentieth century, including Havelock Ellis and Sigmund Freud, revealed the possibility of women's passion and sexuality.

But whether the women had sex or not is irrelevant. They lived in what Blanche Wiesen Cook terms a homosocial world. The women identified with women, loved women, and chose to live their lives with other women. In an era that downplayed women's sexuality, we can hardly categorize them by twentieth-century definitions.

1. LADY ELEANOR BUTLER and SARAH PONSONBY, "The Ladies of Llangollen," b. 1739 and 1755, Irish gentlewomen
Butler and Ponsonby became passionately attached in school and eloped twice before they succeeded in convincing their wealthy Irish families to let them live together. They settled in Wales and lived on a small allowance from the family. As typical

gentlewomen, they spent their days gardening, drinking tea, entertaining, and writing letters.

During their fifty-three years together, they became so famous that they were admired by many notables of the day, including Sir Walter Scott, William Wordsworth, and the duke of Wellington. They also became a shining example of the romantic ideal for many other women.

2. MME. DE LA FAYETTE, author of *The Princess of Cleves*, and supposed lover of both LA ROCHEFOUCAULD and MME. DE SÉVIGNÉ, seventeenth-century Frenchwoman whose letters are a landmark of the epistolary genre.

3. KATHERINE PHILIPS, 1631-1664, English poet known as "the matchless Orinda," and ANNE OWEN

4. MME. DE STAËL, 1776-1817, French novelist, and MME. JULIE RÉCAMIER, patron of the arts. Récamier's name was linked to Chateaubriand, but she was said to have only had platonic relationships with men. De Staël wrote about Récamier in *Corinne*.

5. SARAH SCOTT, eighteenth-century British author, and BARBARA MONTAGU, sister of Lord Halifax

These two lived together until Lady "Bab's" death. During their life together, they founded a charity project for poor girls which Scott wrote about in *A Description of Millenium Hall*.

6. ELIZABETH CARTER, 1717-1806, bluestocking who translated Epictetus, and CATHERINE TALBOT, writer

Although these two never had a chance to live together, neither ever married. Catherine was an invalid who lived at home and Elizabeth cared for her widowed father, a common situation for unmarried women at the time.

Their friendship lasted over thirty years, until Catherine's death. Their early letters are full of protestations of love, sexual tension, and the usual fear in a newfound relationship of revealing too much too soon. The later letters are less intense and full of jealousy, especially after Elizabeth Carter met Elizabeth Montagu.

Montagu was a strong feminist and bluestocking who held literary salons and was called "the Queen of the Blues." Upon the death of her husband, Montagu settled a hundred pounds a year on Carter, an extraordinarily large sum for the time.

7. MARY WOLLSTONECRAFT, eighteenth-century English feminist and author, and FANNY BLOOD

Wollstonecraft and Blood lived together for a time and opened a successful school. But eventually Mary convinced Fanny — who was suffering from consumption and, according to Mary, not strong enough for the emotional rigors of being a woman on her own — to marry a mutual friend who could take her to Portugal for her health.

Even so, Fanny died in Mary's arms. Mary named her first child "Fanny" and wore a locket with Fanny's hair in it until her own death in 1797. She also wrote the 1788 novel *Mary* about her relationship with Fanny.

8. ANNA SEWARD, 1747-1809, British poet, and HONORA SNEYD, a childhood friend

Seward loved Sneyd through Sneyd's marriage and death. The two women lived together until the marriage and Seward wrote poems about Honora until her own death, thirty years later.

9. MARIANNE WOODS and JANE PIRIE, early nineteenth-century English educators

These two women ran a girls' boarding school; the school is remembered today because a lawsuit that resulted from accusations of lesbianism between the two women inspired Lillian Hellman's play, *The Children's Hour*.

In real life, unlike the play, neither women committed suicide as a result of the charge, although their careers *were* ruined. In fact, they ended up successfully suing the woman who spread the rumor. By the end of the legal battles, their life savings were destroyed but not their relationship.

One reason they won in court was lesbian invisibility. The judge said it was "preposterous" and unbelievable that two middle-class women would have sex with each other.

10. ANNA COGSWELL WOOD and IRENE LEACHE, nineteenth-century England

Little is known of these two women except what Anna wrote in her memoirs, but they spent over thirty years together in what was otherwise a marriage. Anna clearly felt they both blossomed as a result of their union.

11. GERALDINE JEWSBURY, nineteenth-century English writer and feminist, and JANE CARLYLE, wife of Thomas Carlyle

Carlyle apparently took great pleasure in belittling his wife's intellect. Consequently, Jane was one of the many women of the day who escaped being a second-class citizen through the loving eyes and supportive words of another woman.

12. EDITH SOMERVILLE, 1861-1949, and VIOLET MARTIN, nineteenth-century Irish novelists who lived together for over thirty years and wrote under the pen name, "Martin Ross."

13. MARIE CORELLI, 1855-1924, British best-selling novelist, and BERTHA VYVER, a painter, musician, and novelist who gave up her own career to further Corelli's.

14. MLLE. DE SCUDÉRY, 1607-1701, French novelist, and MLLE. PAULET

Madeleine de Scudéry's novels are landmarks in the history of the French novel. She established a famous Paris literary salon, and depicted herself as the character "Sappho" in *Le Grand Cyrus*, adopting that name as a pseudonym. In addition to Mlle. Paulet, she carried on a forty-year close and passionate friendship with a man.

15. OCTAVE THANET, late nineteenth-century American who was one of the highest paid authors of her day, and JANE CRAWFORD

Having been girlhood friends, Thanet and Crawford set up house together after Crawford's short marriage ended in her husband's death. They lived together in a mansion named "Thanford" for the rest of their lives and died within a few years of each other.

16. PATIENCE WHITE and SARAH DOWLING, nineteenth-century American farmers

White and Dowling bought a farm together in Greene County, New York, and lived there for the rest of their lives. Their story was the inspiration for Isabel Miller's wonderful novel *Patience and Sarah.*

17. MARY ANN WILLSON, nineteenth-century artist, and MISS BRUNDIDGE

Little is known about these two women except that they also lived and worked together in Greene County, New York, about the same time as White and Dowling. A good guess is that they were part of an extensive lesbian friendship network of the day.

*This information on romantic friends is taken from *Surpassing the Love of Men,* by Lillian Faderman.

8 Novels about Romantic Friends*

1. *THE WIDE, WIDE WORLD*, Elizabeth Wetherell (1852)

2. *DESPERATE REMEDIES*, Thomas Hardy (1871)

3. *WORK: A STUDY OF EXPERIENCE*, Louisa May Alcott (1873)

4. *DEEPHAVEN*, Sarah Orne Jewett (1877)

5. *AN OLD-FASHIONED GIRL*, Louisa May Alcott (1883)

6. *THE BOSTONIANS*, Henry James (1886)

7. *DIANA VICTRIX*, Florence Converse (1897)

8. *JANET AND HER DEAR PHEBE*, Clarissa Dixon (1909)

*This list is derived from *Surpassing the Love of Men*, by Lillian Faderman.

4 University Women Who Had Romantic Friends

1. M. CAREY THOMAS

The first woman president of Bryn Mawr College, Thomas has many other firsts to her credit, including being the first woman to attend Sage College, Johns Hopkins University, and the Universities of Leipzig and Zurich.

However, it was her relationship with a romantic friend that helped her get the Bryn Mawr post. In 1893, her close friend Mary Garrett promised the college a ten-thousand-dollar-a-year grant if Thomas were given the position. The bequest was to last as long as Thomas remained president and Garrett lived.

During her tenure, Thomas created the world-famous medical college at Johns Hopkins — on the condition that women also be admitted to the school. Thomas's relationship with Mary Garrett and English professor Mamie Gwinn was the inspiration for Gertrude Stein's 1904 novel *Fernhurst*.

2. MABEL HAYNES

Another Bryn Mawr alumna, Haynes was the inspiration for the character "Mabel" in Stein's autobiographical coming-out novel *Q.E.D.* Stein apparently fell in love with May Bookstaver, who was also seeing Haynes at the time, and spent three years involved in a love triangle while trying to sort out her still unresolved feelings about lesbianism.

3. MARY WOOLLEY

The president of Mount Holyoke College, Woolley was named one of the twelve greatest living American women in 1930 and was the only female member of the 1932 Geneva Arms Conference.

She had a long-term relationship with author Jeannette Marks, who wrote *Gallant Little Wales* in addition to twenty other books.

4. KATHERINE LEE BATES

A professor at Wellesley, Bates had a romantic friendship with another faculty member, Katharine Coman. Their relationship is part of the biography *Dream and Deed: The Story of Katherine Lee Bates*, by Dorothy Burgess.

8 Scientists, Mathematicians, Scholars, and Doctors

1. AGNODICE, fourth century B.C., Greece

Agnodice was the first woman gynecologist in recorded history. She disguised herself as a man to attend medical classes, and had to continue the practice to follow her calling. Probably because of her sympathetic bedside manner, she became a popular doctor. But eventually she was charged with corrupting young women; scholars today surmise that male doctors who were envious of her large clientele instigated the accusation.

When it became public at the trial that she was a woman, the charge was reduced to practicing a profession that was restricted to men only, and Agnodice was acquitted.

Whether she was actually a lesbian is not known but like many women who cross-dressed to pursue their goals in a man's world, she should probably be included in the wide pantheon of lesbian foremothers.

2. JAMES MIRANDA BARRY, b. about 1795, England

Little is known about Barry's actual birthdate or the age at which she, the first English woman doctor, enrolled as a medical student at Edinburgh University. She is thought to have become a med student anywhere from the astonishing age of ten to the still-surprising age of fifteen. Whatever her age, she completed her doctorate in two years and immediately enlisted in the Army as a surgeon, where she worked throughout the British colonies for nearly fifty years.

She was also one of the first doctors in the modern Western world to practice preventive medicine.

Barry passed as a man all of her life, although it's thought that some other physicians suspected she was a woman. An autopsy was ordered at her death, during which it was revealed that she was not a man.

3. DR. MARY EDWARDS WALKER, 1823-1919, U.S.

After receiving her medical education, Walker chose to dress as a man to practice her profession with less confinement, a habit she continued for the rest of her life. During the Civil War, she joined the Union Army, worked as a doctor, and was eventually caught behind Confederate lines administering to the general populace.

Although she often dressed as a man both on the job and off, Walker kept her female gender identity by wearing her hair in curls — even with a top hat. She was arrested several times for wearing men's clothes.

Walker later became a journalist and was one of the first women in that field. An ardent feminist, she founded an all-women's colony appropriately called "Adamless Eden."

For her work in the Civil War, she was awarded the Congressional Medal of Honor in 1866 by President Andrew Johnson.

4. SONYA KOVALEVSKY, 1850-1891, Russia

Although refused admission to classes, Kovalevsky was tutored privately and received her doctorate in absentia from the University of Göttingen. After many years of struggle, she was eventually appointed to a post at the University of Stockholm.

Her brilliance was finally recognized and her work in mathematics won the Prix Bordin from the French Academy in 1889. She is remembered today for the Caucy-Kovalevsky theorem of differential equations.

She is less well known for her romantic friendship with Swedish author Anne Charlotte Leffler-Edgren, the duchess of Cajanello. Although Kovalevsky had had a short marriage and bore one daughter, her relationship with Leffler lasted many years. Together, they wrote several books, including *A Struggle for Happiness* about love. The main character of Alice is based on Kovalevsky.

Kovalevsky also wrote popular novels such as *The Private Tutor* and *The Rajevski Sisters* under the pseudonym of "Tanya Rerevski."

5. DR. SARA JOSEPHINE BAKER, 1873-1945, U.S.

Another woman who cross-dressed to practice her profession, Dr. Baker also believed in preventive medicine and was in a position to put her theories to practice. During her years at the New York City Department of Health, the infant mortality rate there became the lowest in the U.S. and Europe.

It was Baker's detective work that led to the capture of Typhoid Mary, a domestic servant who passed the disease to many of her employers before she was apprehended. I.A.R. Wylie's book *My Life with George* describes Wylie's long-lasting love affair with Baker.

6. RUTH BENEDICT, 1887-1948, U.S.

A pioneer in anthropology, Benedict is best known in the lesbian community for her mentor relationship with world-famous anthropologist Margaret Mead. Her writings, like Mead's, were both best-sellers and classics of scholarship. *Patterns of Culture* and *Zuni Mythology* grew out of her work with Native American cultures in the 1920s and early 1930s.

Benedict later analyzed racism in *Race: Science and Politics* in 1940. In an acclaimed later work, *The Chrysanthemum and the Sword*, she applies anthropological methods to the study of Japanese culture.

Although Benedict and Mead were both married, they had what has been called a romantic friendship which started in Mead's student days and lasted much of their lives. The best collection of Benedict's writing was edited by Mead.

7. ALBERTA LUCILLE "ALAN L." HART, b. 1892, U.S.

Alberta Hart began passing as a man at the age of twenty-seven and spent the rest of her life as Alan L. Hart. During that time, she wrote many books on science, such as *These Mysterious Rays* about the new discoveries of radium and X-rays as well as *The Undaunted*, an autobiographical novel.

8. EUGENE C. PERKINS, d. 1936, U.S.

Little is known of Perkins's life except that the male doctor was revealed to be a woman on her death in 1936. Perkins had been married to another woman for twenty-eight years prior to her death.

7 Lesbian Entrepreneurs, Explorers, and Athletes

1. LADY HESTER STANHOPE, b. 1776, England

Called "the last of the English eccentrics," Stanhope was the first British citizen to visit many tribes in North Africa and the Middle East in the early nineteenth century. She spent some years with a much younger man but refused to marry him and took up with Elizabeth Williams instead.

A transvestite in her later years, she claimed that she began wearing men's clothing when she lost her luggage. She eventually bought a convent in Lebanon where she offered refuge to local political prisoners. For many years, she received a government pension courtesy of her uncle, Prime Minister William Pitt the Younger. When it ended, she became a recluse, walled herself up in her convent, and died penniless.

2. ANN BANCROFT, contemporary, U.S.

In 1986, Bancroft became the first woman and the first lesbian to reach the North Pole. In the past, she taught physical education but now works with an organization that takes disabled people on wilderness trips. Bancroft was one of *Ms. Magazine*'s women of the year.

3. LULU, early twentieth century, France

"Lulu," as she has come down to us, owned the most famous gay bar of Paris in the 1930s, the Monocle. Her life is detailed in *The Secret Paris of the Thirties*, by Brassai.

4. SALLY EDWARDS, contemporary, U.S.

An enterpreneur and athlete, Edwards co-founded Fleet Feet, Inc., a company that sells sporting goods, in 1975. Twelve years later, the chain spanned twenty-seven stores and grossed nearly ten million.

Edwards also runs marathons regularly and holds the world record for the women's master's division of the Ironman triathlon.

5. & 6. CONNIE BEST and SOPHIA COLLIER, contemporary, U.S.

These two lesbians founded Soho Sodas, which sells natural sodas and mineral waters, in 1977. Today, their product is distributed worldwide.

7. MARTINA NAVRATILOVA, contemporary, Czechoslovakia

A world-famous tennis champion, Navratilova defected to the U.S. during a tennis tour and tells of the harrowing escape in her autobiography, *Martina.*

In the book, she also discusses her relationships with lesbian novelist Rita Mae Brown and transsexual Renée Richards, who has coached her tennis game.

13 Contemporary Lesbian Ministers, Witches, and Ex-Nuns

1. REV. LEANNA R. ANDERSON
Anderson received bishop status in 1987 and recently became presiding bishop of the Restoration Church of Jesus Christ, a church which serves lesbian and gay Mormons. The church has what are called "families" in Utah, Arizona, California, and Texas.

2. REV. ELLEN BARRETT
Barrett, an Episcopalian, was the first openly gay woman to be ordained as a minister of an American church by any denomination.

3. Z BUDAPEST
A practicing witch who traces her roots back through generations of Hungarian women, Budapest is the author of *The Feminist Book of Light and Shadow*, a how-to of contemporary paganism.

4. & 5. ROSEMARY CURB and NANCY MANAHAN
These two ex-nuns edited the controversial *Lesbian Nuns: Breaking Silence*, a collection of moving accounts of lesbianism in the convent.

6. REV. ROSE MARY DENMAN
Denman had been a strong advocate of gay rights — even supporting the ordination of homosexuals — even before she realized she, too, was gay. When she came out, she lost her post with the United Methodist Church.

7. REV. KIM CRAWFORD HARVIE
In 1989, Boston's historic Unitarian congregation, the Arlington Street Church, voted unanimously to accept Harvie as its first lesbian minister.

8. REV. CARTER HEYWARD
A close friend of Barbara Harris, the first woman to be

consecrated as a bishop in the U.S. by the Episcopal Church, Heyward is an openly gay woman who has long supported gay rights within the seventy-million-member worldwide Anglican religious community.

9. REV. DELORES JACKSON

A black activist-minister who was forced to leave the pulpit for her politics, Jackson founded the Third World Gay Women's Organization and Salsa Soul Sisters, a Hispanic and black lesbian organization.

10. REV. MAGORA E. KENNEDY MILLER

Miller has been kicked out of two churches for political beliefs that are anti-war, anti-male, and pro-woman. At present, she is hoping to establish an all-woman church.

11. REV. FREDA SMITH

Smith was the first woman ordained in the lesbian and gay Metropolitan Community Church. A political activist of nearly three decades, Smith was instrumental in the passage of the California Consenting Adults Bill which gave protection to homosexual acts between consenting adults in the privacy of their homes.

12. SABRINA SOJOURNER

A black lesbian, Sojourner is a designated spiritual leader of the First Existentialist Congregation of Atlanta, a church which is committed to diversity. As such, it honors pagan and Afro-American as well as Judeo-Christian beliefs and holidays.

13. LIVE OAK WOMON

Live Oak Womon is a black pagan who lives on the West Coast but travels across the country to bless lesbian gatherings and preside at celebrations.

8 Holy Days for Lesbians *

These pagan holy days are still celebrated by many lesbians, as well as Christians and people of other religions, many of whom do not realize how many of their religious holidays originated from high points of the pagan year.

In the old days, holy days started in the evening. These high holy days counterpointed the full-moon ritual sabbats or esbats.

1. HALLOWMAS, October 31

For many ancient cultures, the beginning of the new year was celebrated on the eve of October 31. In Celtic worship, Halloween was one of the two great fire festivals.

Even today, it is a time of remembrance, of looking back to one's ancestors, and turning inward to look at oneself. It is a time to contact both the dead and the spirits who guide our lives, and a time of peering into the future through divination.

2. WINTER SOLSTICE, December 21

Held December 25 on the old Julian calendar, this festival was the origin of Christmas.

It is a time to wonder at the cold, sterile beauty of Mother Nature at her most austere, and to think of the annual cycle of aging of the earth's hag or crone self.

It is also a time to celebrate the birth of the sun as the days begin to lengthen and the hours of light to wax. It is generally a family affair which is held indoors. Lighting the Yule log and eating Yule log cakes are holdovers from it.

3. CANDLEMAS, February 2

Shrove Tuesday or Mardi Gras is the modern name for this great festival, in which the participants burned a straw effigy to bury winter and waken the sleeping giant of earth. Many of the world's major carnivals are still held to celebrate this festival. In the past, the carnivals were often part of a period known as "turning everything upside-down" in which celebrants dressed in the clothing of the opposite sex.

4. SPRING EQUINOX, March 21

Bonfires were often kindled on the highest mountain to mark this night, to celebrate the full return of spring with the earth's newly-budding vegetation. Its promise of regeneration led to its adoption by the early Christian Fathers as Easter.

5. MAY EVE, May 1

Known as Beltane Eve among the Celts, this was another great fire festival of the year. It was a celebration of fertility and abundance. Today, children repeat the age-old festival when they dance around a May pole.

6. MIDSUMMER'S EVE, June 21

Summer solstice is probably the most widely practiced pagan ritual still held today, as thousands of sun-worshippers watch the sun set from the beach or the highest mountain peak every year. The longest day of the year, it is a turning point in the earth's annual life.

In ancient times, this evening was celebrated with a huge bonfire, torch processions lit from the bonfire, rolling wheels, cartwheels, and acrobatics.

7. LAMMAS, August 1

Lammas celebrates the goodness of the earth as seen in the grain harvest; a reminder of the days when bread was literally "the staff of life."

8. SAMHAIN, September 21

Today's Thanksgiving comes down to us from this ancient harvest rite of praising the goddess for a bountiful and abundant life.

*This list is derived from *The Feminist Book of Lights & Shadows*, by Z Budapest.

11 Lesbian Queens and Aristocrats

1. CHRISTINA, b. 1626, Sweden

Raised as a boy, Queen Christina chose to abdicate in 1654 rather than marry and bear children for the throne. She was in love with Ebba Sparre, a countess, who left her after the abdication. Christina was also in love with opera singer Angelica Georgini.

2. ANNA MARIE LOUISE D'ORLEANS, seventeenth century, France

Like many aristocrats, the duchess of Montpensier was not above falling in love with a courtesan, the beautiful Ninon de Lenclos.

3. QUEEN ANNE, b. 1665, England

Despite a relatively happy marriage, Queen Anne spent the better part of her emotional life loving women. She had three great loves, the most important of which was Sarah Jennings Churchill, duchess of Marlborough, a friend from adolescence.

Anne was particularly fond of Churchill and her husband and showed her affection by giving them gifts, land, and annuities. One such gift was the estate of Blenheim, where a life-size statue of the queen still stands.

Biographers often use the marriage of both women as a shield to protect them from any hint of women-loving taint. Yet any lesbian who reads about the "unexplainable" screaming quarrels that occurred in public toward the end of their relationship — at a point when Anne had already taken up with Churchill's cousin, Abigail Hill — knows that such behavior makes the most sense if we are talking about lovers, not "friends."

4. MARIE ANTOINETTE, 1755-1793, France

Born in Vienna, Marie Antoinette became queen of France when her husband Louis ascended the throne. She is most famous today for her "Let them eat cake" remark about the breadless poor, which did not help her case when the Revolution came along.

She was as famous in her day, however, for the sexual intrigues of the court and her well-known circle of "Sapphists."

She met her death at the guillotine in 1793.

5. MARIE-LOUISE, eighteenth century, France

The princess de Lamballe, she was alleged to be a lover of Marie Antoinette. She refused to take an oath against the monarchy and was torn to pieces by the Paris mob.

6. YOLANDE-MARTINE GABRIELLE DE POLASTRON, eighteenth century, France

A lover of Marie Antoinette, the duchess de Polignac managed to escape death at the hands of the revolutionaries by fleeing to Russia.

7. MARIA CAROLINE, eighteenth century, France

Marie Caroline also ended up at the French court when her sister, Marie Antoinette, married Louis XVI. Her lovers were said to include Emma Lyon Hamilton, a famous switch-hitter, and Lady Hester Stanhope, an English explorer who dressed as a man and eventually settled in a monastery in the North African desert.

8. MARIA LEOPOLDINA, nineteenth century, Brazil

The daughter of Francis I of Austria, Maria was married off to Pedro I of Brazil and lived unhappily in that foreign country until she met Maria Graham, an English writer.

9. LADY UNA TROUBRIDGE, early twentieth century, England

The lover of Radclyffe Hall for nearly thirty years, she is one of the two women to whom Hall's book *The Well of Loneliness* was dedicated. The other in the dedication "To the three of us" was Veronica Batten, Troubridge's cousin and Hall's other long-term love, who had died several years earlier. Hall and Troubridge were psychic investigators, and believed they were remaining in close touch with Batten through seances. It is the only known case of a *ménage à trois* in which one of the members was dead.

10. ELIZABETH DE GRAMONT, early twentieth century, France

A woman who continued to be a lesbian and wrote voluminous memoirs under her maiden name of de Gramont after she married, the duchesse de Clermont-Tonnerre is now best known for her portrayal in Hall's novel *The Well of Loneliness*.

11. MARIE MADELEINE, early twentieth century, Germany

A German poet, Baroness von Puttkamer wrote poems of lesbian love at a time when few people even mentioned the word.

5 Acts of Adoration —
Lesbians and Amazons on Coins

Having one's portrait on a coin is among the highest honors given to an individual and as such, is usually reserved for kings, queens, and heads of state. Most of the women who appear on coins are mythological creatures such as Ceres (nineteenth-century France) or Athena (throughout the ancient world).

The female image of Victory has been used throughout the Western world from as early as the fifth century B.C. In the U.S. alone, Victory has been pictured with Art Nouveau locks, Grecian coils, a feathered Indian headdress, a revolutionary headwrap, and in full figure with sunburst and arrows.

The date given is the century the coin was minted.

1. SAPPHO, sixth century B.C., Greece

2. GORGONS, fourth century B.C., Greece

3. QUEEN CHRISTINA, seventeenth century, Sweden

4. QUEEN ANNE, eighteenth century, England

5. SUSAN B. ANTHONY, twentieth century, U.S.

18 Acts of Honor — Lesbians and Romantic Friends on Stamps

1. SUSAN B. ANTHONY, American suffragette

2. JEANNE D'ARC, French military leader and saint

3. BETTINE VON ARNIM, German author

4. WILLA CATHER, American novelist

5. CATHERINE THE GREAT, Russian empress

6. CHRISTINA, queen of Sweden

7. EMILY DICKINSON, American poet

8. ANNE FRANK, adolescent Jewish author who was killed by the Nazis during World War II. The unexpurgated edition of her diaries, kept while she hid in an attic during the early years of the war, reveal a passionate adolescent attachment to another young woman.

9. LOUISE MICHEL, French anarchist

10. EDNA ST. VINCENT MILLAY, American poet

11. FLORENCE NIGHTINGALE, English nurse and activist

12. JULIE RÉCAMIER, French patron of the arts

13. ELEANOR ROOSEVELT, American First Lady

14. GEORGE SAND, French novelist

15. MME. DE STAËL, French novelist

16. DR. MARY EDWARDS WALKER, American surgeon

17. EDITH WHARTON, American novelist

18. FRANCES E. WILLARD, American educator

8 Famous People
Who Had Lesbian Relatives

1. A.E. HOUSMAN, 1859-1936, England

A gay poet best remembered today for his 1896 volume *A Shropshire Lad*, a celebration of male youth and beauty, Housman had a playwright sister, Clemence, and a brother, Laurence, who were also gay. Clemence was a renowned engraver who supported Laurence with her work until he began to make a name for himself. She also wrote books which Laurence illustrated, one of which was titled *Werewolves*.

2. HENRY JAMES, 1843-1916, U.S.

An American novelist who is known for intricate works like *Turn of the Screw*, James was pleased when his sister Alice, a recluse beset by ill health, finally found the love of her life in Katharine Loring. James and his family were apparently so pleased with the romantic friendship that he wrote about it in the novel *The Bostonians*.

Lesbian critic Lillian Faderman argues that contemporary literary critics misread the novel because of their negative views of lesbianism. Their heterosexual blinders obscure the fact that the relationship James wrote about was meant to be seen in a positive light, as it was by him and his contemporaries.

3. LYTTON STRACHEY, b. 1880, England

The author of *Eminent Victorians*, one of the first books to take an unbowdlerized, factual look at such Victorian notables as nurse-activist Florence Nightingale, Strachey was himself gay. In his youth, he and Virginia Woolf toyed with the idea of a marriage of convenience but eventually abandoned the idea.

Strachey's sister, Dorothy Strachey Bussy, did marry, but that didn't stop her from having love relationships with women and putting it on paper. She wrote an anonymous memoir of her lesbianism under the pseudonym "Olivia" and also translated the gay French author, André Gide, into English.

4. OSCAR WILDE, b. 1856, Ireland

Wilde, the most famous person ever arrested for homosexuality in England, also had a gay niece, Dolly. She, too, was a well-known wit of her day and was said to look exactly like Oscar. She had a tumultous relationship with Natalie Barney for over a decade.

5. EDWARD HYDE, LORD CORNBURY, d. 1723, England

The colonial governor of New Jersey, New York, and North Carolina, a cousin of Queen Anne, and a drag queen of the most magnificent sort, Lord Cornbury appears in his official portrait as governor in full, feminine regalia. His cousin — the real queen — was known for her long-term love relationships with Sarah Churchill, duchess of Marlborough, and Abigail Hill, Lady Masham.

6. E.F. BENSON, early twentieth century, England

Famed for his Mapp and Lucia series of comic novels, E.F. had a mother and two sisters who were lesbian.

After having six children, his mother, Mary "Minnie" Sedgwick Benson, left her husband, the archbiship of Canterbury, for Lucy Tait, the daughter of the previous archbishop. She and Tait then left England for a life on the island of Lesbos.

Benson's sister Nellie was a noted figure in London's artistic circles of the 1920s and a close friend of English composer and suffragist Dame Ethel Smyth.

Benson's other sister, Maggie, led the British excavation of the Temple of Mut in Karnak and was a prolific writer.

7. SIR OSBERT SITWELL, b. 1892, England

Osbert was famed for his wit and his essays on such subjects as architecture, painting, and music. The great love of his life was David Horner.

His sister, noted poet Dame Edith Sitwell, was also gay. She too inherited the family's sense of humor, was a wit of her day, and loved to accentuate her great height by dressing up in striking hats.

8. COLLEY CIBBER, 1671-1757, England

Cibber provided the inspiration for Alexander Pope's satire, *The Dunciad*, but in his day, he was also a well-known playwright, actor, and theater manager. But, as with everyone in the theater, he was hardly considered respectable. In the seventeenth century, theater people were one step above ruffians, thiefs, and prostitutes.

Cibber's daughter, actress Charlotte Charke, was a well-known eccentric and lesbian-transvestite who passed as a man and married other women a number of times. She wore male clothing from the age of four and wrote an autobiography.

Although other women of the day were arrested for transvestism, Charke was probably allowed to live peacefully — and even make money on her habits — because of her occupation and family name.

19 Historical Lesbian Couples and Their Years Together

Despite the stereotype of gay relationships as short-lived, many lesbian couples past and present have spent the major part of their lives together.

One such couple, Katherine Bradley and Edith Cooper — who were aunt and niece — lived the whole of their lives together. They grew up together, moved in with each other as adults, and created a career, writing books under the shared pen name of "Michael Field." They even died within a few years of each other.

1. ROMAINE BROOKS and
   NATALIE BARNEY, 53 years

2. GERTRUDE STEIN and
   ALICE B. TOKLAS, 39 years

3. SYLVIA BEACH and
   ADRIENNE MONNIER, 20 years

4. OCTAVE THANET and
   JANE CRAWFORD, 50 years

5. MAZO DE LA ROCHE and
   CAROLINE CLEMENT, 75 years

6. LADY ELEANOR BUTLER and
   SARAH PONSONBY, 53 years

7. EDITH HAMILTON and
   DORIS FIELDING REID, 60 years

8. MARY WOOLLEY and
   JEANNETTE MARKS, 52 years

9. RADCLYFFE HALL and
LADY UNA TROUBRIDGE, 27 years

10. ANNA COGSWELL WOOD and
IRENE LEACHE, 30 years

11. MAUD HUNT SQUIRE (MISS FURR) and
ETHEL MARS (MISS SKEENE), 20 years

12. TINY DAVIS and
RUBY LUCAS, 42 years and counting...

13. ROSA BONHEUR and
NATHALIE MICAS, 40 years

14. MARY RENAULT and
JULIE MULLARD, 50 years

15. DAME IVY COMPTON-BURNETT and
MARGARET JOURDAIN, 30 years

16. SARAH ORNE JEWETT and
ANNIE FIELDS, 30 years

17. WILLA CATHER and
EDITH LEWIS, 40 years

18. CHARLOTTE CUSHMAN and
EMMA STEBBINS, 20 years

19. H.D. (HILDA DOOLITTLE) and
BRYHER, 40+ years

1 Lesbian Couple in the Bible

Recent interpretations of Ruth and Naomi's relationship have led lesbian and gay scholars to conclude that their love was quite different from the traditional relationship of mother-in-law and daughter-in-law. When Naomi tries to make Ruth go back to her own family on the death of Ruth's husband, Ruth refuses, choosing instead to follow the widow Naomi to her homeland. Once with Naomi's people, Ruth even bears a child for Naomi.

A popular refrain of love — often used in wedding ceremonies — comes from the book of Ruth, Chapter 1, verses 16 and 17. Ruth is speaking to Naomi:

> Whither thou goes, I will go
> Where thou lodgest, I will lodge
> Thy people shall be my people
> Thy God my God
> Where thou diest, will I die
> And there I will be buried
> The Lord do so to me and more also,
> If aught but death part thee and me.

3 Lesbian Couples
Buried with Each Other

1. ROSA BONHEUR and NATHALIE MICAS
Bonheur and Micas lived together most of their lives and are today buried together in Père Lachaise Cemetery, Paris.

2. GERTRUDE STEIN and ALICE B. TOKLAS
Like any other married couple, Stein and Toklas are together in Père Lachaise, two of the few Americans who have ever been buried in that revered French cemetery.

3. MARJORIE FAITH BARNARD and FLORA ELDERSHAW
These two twentieth-century Australian women — both born in 1897 — shared a flat during much of their lives, wrote novels under the shared pen name M. Barnard-Eldershaw, and are today buried together.

11 Lesbians Who Died Young

1. DOLLY WILDE, 1899-1941

An early twentieth-century English wit, niece of Oscar Wilde, and lover of Natalie Barney, Wilde died at age forty-one of cancer.

2. BESSIE SMITH, 1898-1937

The woman who made blues accessible to the masses, Smith died in her late thirties after being severely injured in a car crash. According to some reports, she was denied treatment at a "whites-only" hospital and hemorrhaged to death when she finally got to a hospital that would treat blacks.

3. LORRAINE HANSBERRY, 1930-1965

A black American poet and playwright best known for her play *A Raisin in the Sun*, Hansberry died of cancer at the age of thirty-five, cutting off what would have been an even more luminous literary career.

4. RENÉE VIVIEN, 1877-1909

A British poet, Vivien lived in Paris and took Baudelaire's decadent classic, *Les Fleurs de Mal*, to heart by living on absinthe, alcohol, and darkness. In her last few years, she became paranoid to the point of madness. She had what appeared to be a master-slave relationship with the incredibly wealthy but closeted Helen Betty Louise Caroline Rothschild, wife of the Baron van Zuylen. Vivien died at thirty-two of long-term, self-induced starvation and drinking. Six years later her beloved but brain-eroding absinthe was outlawed in France.

5. SONYA KOVALEVSKY, 1850-1891

A Russian mathematician, Kovalevsky died at the peak of her career from influenza complicated by pneumonia. She was forty-one.

6. FLANNERY O'CONNOR, 1925-1964

A novelist, O'Connor died of the debilitating disease of lupus at thirty-nine. The many years she suffered from its ravages influenced her work and gave her a special sense of the preciousness of life.

7. KAROLINE VON GÜNDERODE, early nineteenth century

A German poet, von Günderode committed suicide at age twenty-five after the breakup of her relationship with Bettine von Arnim. Their correspondence still survives.

8. ADAH ISAACS MENKEN, 1835-1868

An American actress and poet best known for the Sapphic volume *Infelicia*, Menken died in Paris at age thirty-three.

9. MARGARET FULLER, 1810-1850

An American feminist and educator, Fuller was forty when she was shipwrecked and died at sea just hours before she would have landed in New York.

10. LILI BOULANGER, 1893-1918

A French composer and the first woman to win the Prix de Rome, Boulanger died at twenty-five.

11. LIZ MAREK, d. 1988

A contemporary American musician who founded the lesbian fifties band Cherry Cokes, Liz Marek was one of the 259 people who died on December 21, 1988, when a terrorist bomb exploded on Pan Am flight 103. The long-time peace activist was thirty years old.

7 Lesbians Who Lived to a Ripe Old Age

1. ALICE B. TOKLAS, wife and editor of Gertrude Stein, 89

2. EDITH SOMERVILLE, novelist, 91

3. ANNA DICKINSON, suffragist and feminist orator, 90

4. NATALIE BARNEY, patron of the arts, 95

5. ROMAINE BROOKS, painter, 96

6. JEANNETTE FOSTER, author of the monumental work, *Sex Variant Women in Literature*, 97

7. E.M. "MONTE" PUNSHON
   At 105 years of age, Punshon was chosen to be the spokesperson for Australia's 1988 World Expo because she was thought to be the only Australian still alive who had attended the 1888 Expo. At that point, the media began asking questions about her life and Punshorn revealed her sexual orientation. She said she had known she was a lesbian for nearly a century — since the age of six.
   Punshon died the next year at the age of 106.

"There are fewer ways of making love than they say and more than one believes."
                                        —Renée Vivien, lesbian poet

1 Memorable Love Offering

1. *ORLANDO*, a novel by Virginia Woolf

One of the most beautifully written novels in the English language, Virginia Woolf's *Orlando* was written for her friend and lover, Vita Sackville-West.

A fantasy of the most incredible sort, the novel chronicles the social changes in women's lives from Shakespeare's time to the early twentieth century. It features a central character who changes sex, living first as a man, then as a woman. He-she has love affairs with both sexes. The entire work is a brilliant fictional device for illuminating Vita's very complex nature.

The book is also a tongue-in-cheek tribute — or spoof, depending on your point of view — of Woolf's own father, the noted British intellectual Sir Leslie Stephen.

Although literary historians have questioned whether Vita and Virginia actually had a physical relationship, Vita's letters to her husband and best friend, Harold Nicolson, are quite forthright. Her letter of August 17, 1926 shows her own trepidation in the following words:

"I am scared to death of arousing physical feelings in her, because of the madness. I don't know what effect it would have."

And quite rightly. According to biographers, Virginia had slept with her husband, Leonard, only once after they were married. The incident precipitated a nervous breakdown, and further conjugal relations were abandoned. The fact that Virginia and Leonard were business partners and friends at best was well known at the time. Vita's own relationship with her own homosexual husband had long since resolved itself into a respectful companionship by the time she met Virginia. But, guilt-ridden by her own lesbianism, Vita feared a physical encounter might push Virginia, who was none too stable even at the best of times, over the edge.

Vita did overcome her misgivings, however, and in her letters to Harold, she reveals that the two were going to bed with each other.

Vita's son, Nigel, who later compiled and edited his mother's letters, writes that from Vita's point of view, the physical relationship between the two was tentative at best and not as successful as others Vita had, even though it lasted anywhere from a few months to a year.

Whatever the physical side of the affair, the emotional and intellectual bond was strong. Vita and Virginia were very attached to each other, wrote each other notes daily, and remained close friends for the rest of their lives.

Perhaps most importantly, Virginia wrote lovingly about Vita, her man-woman, leaving us one of the longest — and most readable — celebrations of love ever penned.

5 Torrid Love Affairs

1. VITA SACKVILLE-WEST and VIOLET TREFUSIS, early twentieth-century England

Vita and Violet had a wild three-year romance that took them back and forth across Europe from England to Paris, Monte Carlo, Venice, and Avignon.

Vita had already married Harold Nicolson when she fell in love with Violet. In April 1918, she began leaving Harold for weeks at a time to be with Violet. The two women eventually went to Europe together, traveling for over three months in Paris and Monte Carlo before Vita's guilt got the better of her and she returned to Harold.

When Vita went back to Harold, Violet announced her engagement — apparently out of spite. Vita was overcome with jealousy. She left Harold and returned to Monte Carlo with Violet. A month later, Vita returned to the fold.

Once at home, Vita decided she'd made a mistake and told Harold she was going to elope with Violet. Two weeks later, the women did just that.

By this time, both husbands were starting to be seriously concerned. On Valentine's Day, 1920, they went to Amiens to talk to the women, who gave in and left with their husbands.

That arrangement lasted a month. Vita soon joined Violet in Avignon; the husbands realized there was little they could do, short of chaining the two women up.

Vita and Violet continued to see each other freely from then on but even without the complication of husbands, their relationship continued to be wracked by guilt and emotional difficulties. After more than a year, it gradually broke off.

2. DELIA PERKINS and IDA PRESTON, nineteenth-century America

Delia Perkins cut off her hair with the idea of selling it to obtain money for herself and Ida so the two could run away together in 1893. They were caught soon thereafter and returned to their families in Indianapolis. Unfortunately, history has not recorded what happened to their relationship after that.

3. CLARA DIETRICH and ORA CHATFIELD, nineteenth-century America

Clara was the 28-year-old postmistress and general store-keeper of Pitkin County, Colorado, when her uncle, the Honorable I.W. Chatfield, tried to separate her from her cousin Ora. Even though Ora was only fifteen years old, she knew what she wanted. The two women eloped in 1889.

4. RENÉE VIVIEN and NATALIE BARNEY, early twentieth-century France

Like Vita and Violet, Renée and Natalie had a tempestuous, on-again, off-again relationship, though there were no husbands to complicate matters. There was something worse — other women. Natalie was notorious for her love affairs. For all her feminism, she despised monogamy and conducted intense sexual affairs whether she was seriously involved with anyone else or not.

Renée and Natalie were attracted to each other mentally as well as physically by a shared belief in feminism. They were two of the first truly modern lesbians who used a political analysis to root their sexual preference in women's rights.

Their relationship lasted less than five years but it was productive for each. During that time, they both wrote books with lesbian themes and together attempted to start all-women artist's colonies in Paris and Lesbos.

Renée eventually tired of the sexual intrigues and left Natalie for the Baroness van Zuylen. After attempting to win Renée back, Natalie eventually found the painter, Romaine Brooks. She spent almost all the rest of her life with Romaine, but Romaine also grew weary of the "passing fancies," as she called them, and after fifty-three years together, Romaine cut off the relationship a few years before her own death.

5. LADY ELEANOR BUTLER and SARAH PONSONBY, eighteenth-century Ireland

Sixteen years' age difference and the power of two titled families couldn't stop Eleanor and Sarah from committing themselves to each other when Sarah reached a marriageable age.

They eloped and were brought back the first time — to the great relief of the family, who initially thought Sarah had been kidnapped by a man and were worried about her virginity. Little did they know that Eleanor was a much more formidable foe.

The families tried to keep them apart but a servant, Martha Caryll, passed notes and messages between them until they were finally able to escape. Known as "Molly the Bruiser," Martha went with them on their second attempt. Like Eleanor, Molly was very masculine — a desirable trait at a time when women traveling alone often resorted to men's clothing for protection.

When the families realized they were beaten, they insisted the women leave Ireland but gave them the money to do so. Together with Molly, the women set up house in Wales and became quite well known in their day.

10 Questions
Most Commonly Asked of Lesbians —
and the Answers You'll Never Hear*

1. *What, exactly, do two women do together?* (Usually asked by a woman.)

A: It takes too long to explain. A lesbian quickie lasts hours. We lay there and discuss politics until we figure it out. But if you like I'll show you. How about this evening at six?

2. *Which one of you is the man?* (Usually asked by a man.)

A: We're lesbian, not confused. Look it up!

3. *What do your parents think about it?*

A: They weren't exactly tickled lavender.

4. *Do you face any discrimination because you're — "that way"?*

A: None. The lesbian movement is a bodily function that involves the expulsion of our reproductive organs.

5. *Why are you a lesbian?*

A: Let me show you a picture of my girlfriend.

6. *Did anything in your childhood affect your "choice"?*

A: Definitely. There was this cute little redhead in my nursery school that I used to take naps with...

7. *Why do you have to tell everyone?*

A: I have a P.C. quota to meet.

8. *Is one of you "butch" and the other "femme"?*

A: Yes, but we trade off every time we roll over.

9. *Do you plan to have children?*

A: We're trying! (Wink-wink, nudge-nudge, know what I mean, know what I mean!)

10. *But wouldn't you want your children to be straight?*

A: And miss this opportunity to be interrogated by the next generation of psych majors?

*Courtesy of Chris Lanter and the Gay and Lesbian Students Union Speakers Committee of the University of New Mexico.

14 Epithets for Lesbians

1. ANDROMANIAC, 1890s, meaning a woman who apes men

2. BULL DIKE, 1920s

3. SAPPHIST, 1920s

4. NEW WOMAN, 1930s

5. KIKI, 1940s

6. DIESEL DYKE, 1940s

7. COLLAR-AND-TIE, 1940s

8. SLACKS, 1940s

9. MAJOR, 1940s, as in P.E. major or Army major

10. MANTEE, 1940s

11. AMY-JOHN, 1950s, as in Amazon

12. DERRICK, 1960s

13. JASPER, 1960s

14. LAVENDER MENACE, early 1970s

16 Euphemisms for Lesbians and Lesbian Relationships

1. SMASHES

2. SENTIMENTAL FRIENDS

3. SPECIAL FRIENDS

4. ROMANTIC FRIENDS

5. TWO HEARTS IN COUNSEL

6. LOVE OF KINDRED SPIRITS

7. BOSTON MARRIAGE

8. URNINGIN

9. GYNANDER

10. VIRAGINT

11. INVERT

12. CONTRASEXUAL

13. ANDROGYNE

14. MODERNE

15. ROARING GIRL

16. FEMALE ADVENTURER

12 International Words for Lesbian

1. DONNA CON DONNA, woman with woman, Italian

2. MÄDCHEN SCHMEKER, girl-taster, German

3. MAL-FLOR, tomboy (with negative connotations), Spanish

4. MANFLORA, tomboy, Spanish

5. MARIMACHO, masculine Mary, Spanish

6. PANTALONUDA, tomboy, or wears pants, Spanish

7. POLONE-HOMI, young man, British from Spanish

8. SAWA LINAA, to live as partners, Klamath tribe

9. SHUANG CHIEH, sworn sisters, Chinese

10. SHU NII, self-combers, Chinese

11. TORTILLERA, tortilla maker, Mexican

12. VRILLE, a gimlet, French

20 Native-American Words for Women Berdache *

1. BRUMAIWI (Atsugwewi)

2. SAKWO'MAPI AKIKWAN (Blackfeet)

3. WARHAMEH (Cocopa)

4. KOSKALAKA (Dakota)

5. NTALHA (Flathead)

6. ICKOUE NE KOUSSA (Illinois)

7. CHELXO-DELEAN(E) (Ingalik)

8. TW!INNA'EK (Klamath)

9. TITQATTEK (Kutenai)

10. KWIRAXAME' (Maricopa)

11. HWAMI (Mojave)

12. NÁDLEEH (Navajo)

13. MORONI NOHO (Northern Paiute)

14. OKITCITAKWE (Ojibwa)

15. TAWKXWA'-NSIXW (Quinault)

16. SINTA'-XLAU'WAM (Sanpoil)

17. NUWUDUKA, WAIPPU OR SUNGWE (Shoshoni)

18. MUSP-IWAP NAIP (Ykui)

19. KWE'RHAME (Yuma)

20. KATSOTSE (Zuni)

*This information is taken from the book *Living the Spirit*, edited by Will Roscoe.

9 Ways that Early Twentieth-Century Newspaper Reviews of Broadway Plays Got Around Saying the "L" Word

1. "A TWISTED RELATIONSHIP," *New York Times*, 1926

2. "A WARPED INFATUATION," *New York Times*, 1926

3. "TORMENTING IMPULSES," *World*, 1926

4. "BONDAGE," *World*, 1926

5. "THE POISONOUS SERPENT'S SPELL OF A DECADENT WOMAN," *Evening World*, 1926

6. "A CANCEROUS GROWTH," *Daily News*, 1926

7. "A MONSTROUS SEXUAL PERVERSION," *New York Evening Journal*, 1934

8. "L—N," *New York Herald Tribune*, 1934

9. "A NAUGHTY WORD," *New York Herald Tribune*, 1934

20 Turn-of-the-Century "Ways to Tell" if a Girl Would Become Gay or if a Woman Was a Lesbian — from Medical Journals of the Day

1890s:

1. SMOKES CIGARETTES IN PUBLIC

2. HAS A CAPACITY FOR ATHLETICS AND AN INCAPACITY FOR NEEDLEWORK AND OTHER DOMESTIC OCCUPATIONS (Noted sexologist Dr. Havelock Ellis contributed these observations.)

1895:

3. TOMBOY HABITS

4. DRESSES IN BOYS' CLOTHING

5. ABANDONS DOLLS AND GIRLFRIENDS FOR MARBLES AND MASCULINE GAMES

1900:

6. PREFERS THE LABORATORY TO THE NURSERY

7. GOES TO BARS

8. IS ANTI-SOCIAL

9. HAS A FIRMNESS TO HER WALK, A LONG STEP, AND A RATHER HEAVY TIMBRE TO HER VOICE

10. TALKS LOUD AND USES SLANG

11. HAS AN ENLARGED CLITORIS (Which usually stemmed from "self-abuse," as masturbation was then called.)

12. HAS NO BREASTS TO SPEAK OF

13. IS SQUARE-SHOULDERED AND SOLID

1910:

14. HAS A STRONG, SELF-ASSURED LOOK IN HER EYE

15. SHOWS MENTAL ARROGANCE AND IS ABNORMALLY DEFICIENT IN NATURAL FEMALE SHYNESS

16. IS COLD AND UNEMOTIONAL

17. HAS INTELLECTUAL ATTRIBUTES USUALLY ASSOCIATED WITH MEN — AN ACUTENESS OF COMPREHENSION AND LUCID OBJECTIVITY (We can thank Freud — who also classified lesbians into "butch" and "femme" categories — for this one.)

1912:

18. WEARS STRAIGHT, TAILORED HATS AND HEAVY SHOES

19. DOESN'T WEAR CORSETS

1921:

20. HAS BOBBED HAIR

18 Alleged Causes of Lesbianism

1. MASTURBATION (1600s through early 1900s)

2. FAULTY NERVOUS ORGANIZATION, WHICH CAN ALSO LEAD TO DEMENTIA AND DEATH (1890s)

3. CEREBRAL ABNORMALITIES (1890s)

4. FEAR OF PREGNANCY (1890s)

5. FEMALE FRIENDSHIPS (1890s)

6. BEING ALLOWED TO DRESS LIKE BOYS (1890s)

7. BEING ALLOWED TO PLAY WITH BOYS (1890s)

8. FEMINISM (1890s)

9. SEPARATE SCHOOLS FOR GIRLS AND BOYS (1890s)

10. WOMEN'S COLLEGES WHICH ENCOURAGED ATHLETICS AND THE "MASCULINIZATION" OF THE FEMALE MIND (1900s)

11. CO-ED COLLEGES (1900s)

12. CHILDHOOD TRAUMA (1920s)

13. BEING AN ONLY CHILD OR THE FIRST-BORN (1920s)

14. SHORTAGE OF MEN FOLLOWING WORLD WAR I (1920s)

15. WORLD WAR I: EMOTIONAL TRAUMA CAUSED BY THE SEPARATION OF MEN AND WOMEN DURING THE WAR AND ALSO, WOMEN TAKING OVER MEN'S JOBS (1920s)

16. OVERFUNCTIONING ADRENAL GLAND (1930s)

17. GLANDULAR IMBALANCE (1950s)

18. POOR PARENTING (1960s)

19 Alleged Cures for Lesbianism and Masturbation

1. BROMIDES (1860s)

2. BATHS AND DOUCHES (1880s)

3. OÖPHERECTOMY (REMOVAL OF THE OVARIES) (1880s)

4. VISITING A SPA (1880s)

5. BREAD AND WATER (1890s)

6. CLITORIDECTOMY (REMOVAL OF CLITORIS) (1890s)

7. ANAPHRODISIACS (1890s)

8. EARLY STRESS ON SEXUAL DIFFERENCES (1900s)

9. MAKING LITTLE GIRLS WEAR DRESSES (1900s)

10. CONFINING CHILDREN TO THE COMPANY OF THEIR OWN SEX (1900s)

11. CO-ED EDUCATION (1910s)

12. SEPARATE BEDS (1910s)

13. REST (1910s)

14. SLEEPING WITH THE HANDS INSIDE THE BLANKET (1910s)

15. SITTING ON YOUR FEET (1910s)

16. SURGERY ON THE ADRENAL GLAND (1930s)

17. HORMONES (1930s)

18. ANALYSIS (1920s through 1970s)

19. ISOLATION OR CONFINEMENT TO MENTAL HOSPITAL (1920s through 1970s)

13 Once-Popular Myths about Female Sexuality*

1. A WOMAN'S WOMB IS NOT STATIONARY but travels throughout her body. If it gets lodged in her throat, she will die of suffocation.

2. EDUCATION FORCES TO THE BRAIN BLOOD that is meant for menstruation.

3. WOMEN HAVE NO ACTIVE PART IN THE REPRODUCTIVE PROCESS; they are merely vessels for a man's child. The sperm carries a miniature child, whole and complete, into the woman's body. With the help of primitive microscopes, early scientists actually saw these "little men" and confirmed this "fact" in the late seventeenth century.

4. WOMEN PRODUCE SEMEN which, if retained, causes hysteria, mental illness, and depression, as well as physical aches and pains.

5. WOMEN WILL SPOIL HAM if they try to cure it while menstruating.

6. WOMEN WHO ENJOY SEX will bear retarded or deformed children.

7. WOMEN DO NOT ENJOY SEX.

8. WOMEN ARE INCAPABLE OF ORGASM.

9. A SINGLE ORGASM IS MORE DEBILITATING for a woman than a hard day's work.

10. TOO MUCH INTERCOURSE will cause a woman to be frigid, infertile, and insane; it will create miscarriages, and drive her

to murder her children. It also causes brain tumors, breast cancer, and blood poisoning.

11. MENOPAUSE IS NATURE'S WAY of ending a woman's sex life. Any sexual activity after menopause, even masturbation, can result in serious injury to health.

12. LESBIANS ARE MEN TRAPPED IN A WOMAN'S BODY. Because of the terrible frustration this causes, they are more prone to commit murder and other violent crimes.

13. CUNNILINGUS CAUSES CANCER OF THE TONGUE.

*This list was supplied courtesy of Leigh W. Rutledge.

7 Masturbatory Objects, Real or Alleged

1. THE DEVIL
Despite an icy-cold organ, the devil was popular with lurid minds in the fourteenth through seventeenth centuries.

2. MALE DEMONS
Known as incubi, these spirits could have sex with v omen and make them pregnant — and could also possess them. The idea originated in France during the ninth century but became a vivi ᴀ part of the European witch hunts five centuries later.

3. SEWING-MACHINE PEDALS
An 1869 medical journal warned factory supervisors to look for women who were pedaling too fast.

4. HORSES AND SADDLES
Riding has long been thought to ruin virginity. Besides, it's considered way too much fun by people who would rather little girls sat quietly at home.

5. DOORKNOBS
Part of modern mythology, doorknobs go along with Coke bottles (1950s) and hairbrush handles.

6. DILDOES
One of the few actual masturbatory objects, dildoes have been made from almost every imaginable material over the centuries, including leather with pigs' bladders tied to the end, wood, and ivory. Even a phallus-shaped plant, which when soaked in water hardens and becomes stiff, has been used.

7. RIN-NO-TAMA BELLS
These Oriental inventions originally consisted of two silver balls, one with a drop of mercury inside and the other with a tiny metal tongue that vibrated. When placed in the vagina, the slightest movement of the hips created an erotic sensation. These toys were first brought to Europe in the eighteenth century. The modern version has three bells.

18 Alleged Effects of Masturbation

Seventeenth Century:

1. GOUT

2. CONSTIPATION

3. HALITOSIS

4. RED NOSE

5. HUNCHBACK

6. SWAYBACK

Eighteenth Century:

7. BACKACHE

8. ITCHING

9. NUMBNESS OF THE HANDS

10. VOMITING

11. NYMPHOMANIA

12. INFERTILITY

13. DISTENDED CLITORIS

14. DEATH

Nineteenth Century:

15. BLINDNESS

16. EPILEPSY

Early Twentieth Century:

17. ACNE

18. BRAIN DAMAGE

6 Lesbian Sex Theorists, Sex Radicals, and Erotic Writers

1. TEE CORINNE
Also known as a photographer, Corinne has published a wide variety of erotic books such as *Labiaflowers, Yantras*, and *Dreams of the Woman Who Loved Sex*.

2. JO ANNE LOULAN
Loulan is a sex therapist and lecturer who has published *Lesbian Passions: Loving Ourselves and Each Other* as well as *Lesbian Sex*.

3. SUSIE BRIGHT
Bright founded the erotic lesbian magazine *On Our Backs* in the early 1980s and edited a collection of woman-oriented studies, *Herotica*. She is also known as "Susie Sexpert" for her column on sex toys.

4. PAT CALIFIA
Despite continual run-ins with censors, Califia keeps writing. Her books on sex include *Sapphistry: The Book of Lesbian Sexuality* and *Macho Sluts*. She also writes an advice column for the national gay magazine, *The Advocate*.

5. BERTHA HARRIS
With Emily L. Sisley, novelist Harris also wrote one of the earliest lesbian sex manuals, *The Joy of Lesbian Sex*.

6. MARIANA VALVERDE
The author of *Sex, Power and Pleasure*, Valverde is a theorist who addresses issues such as pornography and sadomasochism, which have split apart the lesbian-feminist community.

9 Poetic Chinese Terms for Female Genitalia from Han Dynasty Marriage Manuals (206 B.C.-A.D. 26)

Each term represents a particular part of the genitals.

1. RED PEARL

2. JADE GATE

3. GOLDEN LOTUS

4. PEONY BLOSSOM

5. CINNABAR GATE

6. GOLDEN CLEFT

7. JADE VEINS

8. JEWEL TERRACE

9. EXAMINATION HALL

11 Clinical Terms
for Sex Acts and Toys That You May Not Find in Webster's Dictionary

1. ALGOLAGNIA, pleasure inseparable from pain

2. COPROLALIA, sexually explicit language during sex

3. CUNNILINGUS, oral sex

4. FROTTAGE, belly-rubbing

5. GERONTOPHILIA, a sexual interest in older people

6. GODEMICHE, use of a dildo

7. MÉNAGE À TROIS, sex among three partners

8. OLISBOS, a dildo

9. SOIXANTE-NEUF, mutual simultaneous oral sex

10. TRIBADISM, genital rubbing (also: lesbianism)

11. TROILISM, a threesome

23 Trash Terms for a Woman's Genitals *

1. BOX
2. BUSH
3. COOZY
4. CUNT
5. FRONT DOOR
6. GARDEN
7. GASH
8. GATE OF HEAVEN
9. GROTTO OF VENUS
10. HONEY POT
11. LOVE BOX
12. LOVE CANAL
13. MUFF
14. OVEN
15. PUSSY
16. QUIM
17. SLIT
18. SNAPPER
19. SNATCH
20. STEAMBOX
21. TREASURE BOX
22. TWAT
23. VASE

*This list was supplied courtesy of Leigh W. Rutledge.

17 Words Beginning with "S"*

1. SACRED, as in her sacred places

2. SAFE, as in within her arms

3. SALTY, as in her skin on a hot summer night

4. SAMPLE, as in her wares

5. SASSY, as in her tongue

6. SAUNTER, as in her walk

7. SECLUSION, as in pine forest

8. SECOND, as in orgasm

9. SEEING, as in believing

10. SEIZE, as in the moment

11. SHEEPISH, as in the first time

12. SHIRT, as in open to the waist

13. SIESTA, as in afterwards

14. SIN, as in no, it's not

15. SKILLED, as in yes, she is

16. SPEECHLESS, as in sometimes afterwards

17. SPINNING, as in circles and circles

*Reprinted with permission of the author, who goes by the sobriquet, "Connie Linguist."

32 Herbs Said to Be Aphrodisiacs

No herb should be taken in large quantities without medical supervision. Their potency can vary greatly between batches, and few herbs have been subjected to modern methods of testing for side effects. Sassafras, for centuries a very popular herbal tea, was eventually tested and found to be a powerful carcinogen. Only the proper part of the herb should be used, and no herb should be used simply because it is listed here.

1. ANEMONE*
2. ARTICHOKE
3. BARBERRY
4. CALAMUS
5. CARLINE THISTLE
6. CELERY
7. CLOVE
8. CORIANDER
9. EUROPEAN VERVAIN
10. FENUGREEK
11. GALANGAL
12. GINGER
13. GINSENG
14. JASMINE
15. JOHIMBE
16. JUNIPER**
17. LADY'S MANTLE
18. LOVAGE**
19. MAIDENHAIR FERN*

20. MATICO

21. MEXICAN DAMIANA

22. NASTURTIUM

23. PANSY*

24. PARSLEY

25. PERIWINKLE*

26. PRICKLY ASPARAGUS

27. QUEEN OF THE MEADOW

28. SAFFRON*

29. SARSAPARILLA

30. SAVORY

31. SAW PALMETTO

32. VALERIAN

*Used in oils for baths or for massage only. Not to be taken internally.

**As emmenagogues, both juniper and lovage promote the onset of menstruation and should not be used by pregnant women or those with kidney problems.

8 Common Foods
Said to Be Aphrodisiacs *

1. CHOCOLATE

2. CRABS

3. EGGS

4. HONEY

5. LETTUCE

6. MUSSELS

7. ONIONS

8. SNAILS

*This information is taken from *Sex in History*, by Reay Tannahill.

11 Bisexual, Transsexual, Hermaphrodite, or Lesbian Plants and Animals

1. JACK-IN-THE-PULPIT

Like some animals, this plant changes from male to female as it matures. The young plant has a male flower and one leaf. After it has grown over the years to around fifteen inches in height, it produces more leaves and a female blossom. Seed production requires much more energy than pollen production; with this strategy the plant postpones seeding until it can afford the energy expenditure.

2. DOLPHINS

Dolphins are perhaps the most sexually liberated species on earth — and some claim the most intelligent. Even though they do not become sexually mature until five years old, they begin to have sex at a few months of age. They practice heterosexual and homosexual lovemaking — and they masturbate with objects such as streams of water gushing into a tank, or their trainers.

3. LYRE-TAIL CORAL FISH or ORANGE SEA PERCH

A shallow-water tropical fish, the largest female will change to a male if the male of the family group is removed or dies. She assumes gaudy coloring, becomes larger, and grows longer fin spines and streamers. This phenomenon, protogyny, occurs in several species of territorial reef fishes.

4. TEN-SPIKED STICKLEBACK

This fish will perform courtship roles of the opposite sex while in captivity even though it does not actually change sex. The female will act as a male to another female and vice-versa, but the eggs won't be fertilized.

5. OYSTERS

Sometimes called an indecisively-sexed bivalve, oysters change sex from male to female — and change back again — on a weekly to annual basis, depending on the species. As with the Jack-in-the-Pulpit, the reason is associated with achieving the maximum number of descendants with available energy resources.

6. SLIPPER LIMPET

This marine snail, known as "crepidula fornicata," also changes sex as it grows. It starts out male, then becomes female if it finds a suitable surface to attach to. It then assures itself of a regular supply of semen by exuding a pheromone which triples the time it takes other limpets in the neighborhood to change to females.

Like many gastropods, slipper limpets hold orgies — only theirs are not of the fleeting one-night-only variety. When a male mounts a female, he becomes permanently attached to her by means of an ingeniously designed penis. He then begins to become — slowly — also female. In the meantime, other limpets arrive and join the party. In a chain, the oldest and largest ones on the bottom are female; those in the middle are in the process of changing; and the smaller ones at the top are still male.

7. BANANA SLUG

Like most molluscs, the slug is a hermaphrodite bisexual that likes orgies in chain or circle formation. In a chain formation, the first slug acts as female; the second as male to the first but female to the next; and so on down the line to the end slug, which only uses the male part of its wonderfully complex anatomy.

8. ROMAN SNAILS

More commonly known as escargot, these hermaphrodites mate face-to-face while standing on their tails. Both play the female and male role simultaneously.

9. PIGEONS

Many birds exhibit homosexuality even when members of the opposite sex are freely available, and pigeons are no exception. They often mate with members of their own sex and form permanent pair bonds. Female couples may lay infertile eggs.

10. RAVENS

Ravens also pair bond, with the dominant female taking the male role in mounting and other activities. The bonds are so strong that females often rebuff male advances. If a male is persistent and able to intrude on the pair, neither female leaves. Instead, the three form a ménage à trois, the male eventually mating with both.

11. GRAYLAG GEESE

Geese usually mate for life — or at least until the death of one. They also exhibit this trait of fidelity when creating a homosexual pair bond. Like ravens, they will form a ménage à trois if a member of the opposite sex can manage to insinuate itself into the family.

These threesomes will not only brood two sets of young, but through the combined strength of three rather than two individuals, they often rise to the top of the flock's pecking order.

5 All-Female Animal Societies

1. DESERT GRASSTAIL or WHIPTAIL LIZARD
This species of lizard, being all-female, not only reproduces by parthenogenesis but also has sex for pleasure.

2. WATER SNAILS
Some species of water snail are hermaphroditic; each snail reproduces autogenetically by using its own penis to fertilize eggs in its own vagina. Other water snails practice parthenogenesis, whereby the eggs develop without being fertilized at all.

3. ELEPHANTS
Long known to live in all-female groups except during musth — the rutting season — elephants are highly intelligent, highly social animals. Recent research has indicated that they know each other personally and communicate over great distances with calls which are below the range of human hearing. If a mother is killed or dies, the other elephants will adopt her calf and rear it.

Like most mammals, elephants masturbate. Primates use hands, feet, mouth, and tail, while dogs and cats make use of their mouths. Since elephants are limited to their trunks — which aren't long enough to reach their genitals — the females masturbate each other. Males do the same during the bulk of their gender-segregated lives.

4. BEES
Male bees exist for only one purpose — to fertilize the queen bee. When one accomplishes this — his sexual apparatus explodes into her vagina, killing him and, by blocking the vagina, assuring that his sperm will have no competition — the other males are simply starved to death.

Once fertilized, the queen bee will not need to mate again for five years, during which time the colony will be an all-female one. In fact, all bees seen collecting nectar in gardens and yards are female — virgin, sterile workers.

5. SPIDERS

Like mockingbirds, spiders live a solitary existence except during the mating season. While male spiders do exist, to the human eye most spiders are female.

Male spiders are commonly much smaller than the females; some are the size of a pinhead, and the untrained observer would assume they are of a different species.

14 Queer and Wonderful Facts about the Animal Kingdom

1. BUTTERFLY

The butterfly has a sexual anatomy as complicated as any creature on earth. It has two vaginas: one used for copulation and another — called an ovipositor — used for eggs.

2. BLUE WHALE

Weighing 175 tons and 100 feet in length, the blue whale is the largest creature on earth and has a vagina to match. Normally some ten feet long, the whale's vagina expands to accommodate a 23-foot blue baby.

3. OCTOPUS

The vagina and penis are recent evolutionary devices which the octopus — like many other creatures — doesn't have. Instead, the female's breathing apparatus (or nose) also acts as a vagina. The male has a hectocotylus — a tentacle slightly longer than the rest that is used to transfer a sperm packet into the female's nose/vagina.

4. CARDINAL FISH

Many lower animals, such as reptiles, crocodiles, fish, and even birds, have what's known as a cloaca — an anus that protrudes to act like a penis for transferring cartridges of sperm, or folds inward and holds eggs to act like a vagina.

The cardinal fish has such a device — except that in this species, the sexes are switched. The cloaca of the female, rather than the male, enlarges. She then uses it to penetrate the male and deposit her eggs in him.

5. SEA HORSE

The female sea horse also takes the male role, using a papilla — or nipple-like projection — as a penis. She takes the initiative in intercourse, releasing eggs into a pouch in the male's belly.

Completing the role reversal, the male then hatches the eggs in his pouch. The pouch grows larger and larger as the young mature until, belly extended, he looks like any other pregnant creature. He eventually gives birth to fully developed, though tiny, baby sea horses.

6. RIVER BULLHEAD

The male of this species of fish plays the female role by making a nest under a rock in a stream bed and enticing the female into it. If she is interested, she will eventually spawn. He will fertilize the eggs, then shoo her out.

He will then spend two weeks fanning the eggs to keep oxygen flowing to them until they hatch. He also protects the young until they are old enough to leave the nest.

7. MOUTH BROODER

The black-chinned mouth brooder of West Africa also practices the custom of couvade — male mimicry of the female birthing process. The male fish incubates the fertilized eggs in his mouth for twenty-three days — during which time he completely abstains from eating.

8. EMPEROR PENGUIN

In this penguin species, the male does all the brooding. He holds the single egg on his feet for two months to protect it from the freezing Antarctic ground until it hatches. When that happens, the female takes over and he goes off for a much-needed chance to fatten up again.

9. BOWERBIRD

The male bowerbird constructs a house (hence the name *bower*) to catch the female's attention. The bowers range from huts to mansions with separate rooms; wall decor can include leaves and flowers, and some bowers even have carpets of colored rocks. Some birds also paint the bower by rubbing berries against the walls, staining them with juice.

In spite of this elaborate show of interest, once the male has accomplished this he leaves the female to build a nest, hatch the eggs, and rear the young by herself.

10. BIRD OF PARADISE

Like many birds, members of the bird-of-paradise family put on a spectacular visual display at courting time. A New Guinea variety engages in a male talent contest in which the female makes her choice on the basis of singing, dancing, and, presumably, overall personality.

11. SPIDERS

Spiders tend to eat anything that moves. Females often eat incautious males during, or instead of, copulation; in many species, the male distracts the female with a silk-wrapped maggot or some equally enticing gift, while he slips in unnoticed. But even if he accomplishes his task and escapes unharmed, he will often stop eating and die afterwards. Once the female lays eggs she, too, will die.

Considering the spiders' considerable reputation for indiscriminate gourmandise, it is only fair to point out that some members of the species — ground and crab spiders — draw the line at cannibalism.

12. PRAYING MANTIS

The female praying mantis also eats the male — in this case, without even waiting for the sex act to get well under way. She begins munching on the male's head as soon as they start copulating and works her way down his body as far as she can reach. Some entomologists believe that this is a necessary part of the act — that an inhibiting gland in the male's head must be disposed of, thus releasing energizing hormones, before copulation can occur at the appropriate frenzied rate — a case of losing one's head over a woman literally as well as figuratively.

13. ANGLER FISH

There are several species of angler fish, but none would win any beauty contests. The females are mostly mouth and teeth and can grow up to five feet long. Their lower fins are modified for walking, but fortunately for land dwellers, these are deep-sea creatures that have never been tempted to evolve onto land.

Anyone studying angler fish females will usually find irregular warts on their bodies. The "warts" are actually minute male anglers which have attached themselves to the female permanently. Once hooked, the female controls the production of semen — the male's sole function — by pumping a hormone through his body. Over time their bloodstreams merge and the male actually melts into her.

Any female who has been tempted to think of men as parasites can see her worst suspicion confimed by this species.

14. HOMO SAPIENS

One question about the human species has never been studied scientifically: parthenogenesis, the production of a child without the assistance of insemination from a male. The case of the Virgin Mary is relevant only if we reject the standard assumption that Jesus was male, as parthenogenetic children are usually female.

Helen Spurway, a noted British scientist, believes it can — and does — happen in the human female. According to Spurway, the incidence is one in 1.6 million pregnancies.

A U.S. research project on parthenogenesis was cancelled because the researchers were inundated by women wanting to participate — and saying they had conceived without any help from the male of the species.

The best-documented recent case occurred in Hanover, Germany, during World War II. Miss Emmie Marie Jones collapsed during a bombing raid. Nine months later she gave birth to a girl although she still claimed to be a virgin. Perhaps the explanation is shock which, in chemical or electric form, can be used to induce parthenogenesis in certain animals.

Except for the age difference, the mother and daughter looked exactly like twins. British geneticists who tested them found that their genetic makeup was identical, and concluded that the case was remarkably like parthenogenesis.

Switch-Hitters
and
Cross-Dressers

14 Famous Switch-Hitters

1. LADY EMMA HAMILTON, 1761-1815, England

A commoner who made her way up the social ladder the hard way, Hamilton was the mistress of both Queen Maria Caroline of Naples and Admiral Nelson.

2. CATHERINE THE GREAT, 1729-1796, Russia

A German princess who deposed her husband and became the Tsar, Catherine hated the female role from an early age. Like many free spirits, she preferred riding and shooting birds to playing with dolls. She wore men's clothes for the freedom it afforded her and led the troops in battle wearing a male uniform.

Her marriage to Tsar Peter III was not consummated for nearly a decade. During that time, she had affairs and was known for her licentiousness. She reputedly had passionate affairs with both women and men.

3. ALLA NAZIMOVA, b. 1879, Russia

The wife of Hollywood director Charles Bryant, Nazimova co-wrote and helped direct the screen version of Wilde's play *Salome*. Another of her earlier movies, *Camille*, included a lesbian scene.

Ken Russell's 1977 camp classic, *Valentino*, includes Leslie Caron as Nazimova.

4. NATASHA RAMBOVA, b. 1897, U.S.

Set and costume designer on *Salome* and other films, Rambova was the wife of silent-screen heartthrob Rudolph Valentino and sometime lover of Alla Nazimova.

5. EDITH LEES ELLIS, twentieth century, England

A writer and lecturer in her own right, Ellis was married to pioneer sexologist Havelock Ellis. She fought for tolerance of "sexual inversion," as homosexuality was then called.

Despite the assumption of heterosexuality because of her marriage to Ellis, she was the subject of one of her husband's most famous case studies of lesbianism.

6. MARGARET MEAD, 1901-1978, U.S.

At the height of her career, Mead was the most widely known anthropologist in the world. She wrote over forty books, the most famous of which is *Coming of Age in Samoa*. Married three times, she is believed by many to have had a romantic attachment with anthropologist Ruth Benedict.

7. ELIZABETH ARDEN, 1878-1966, Canada

Along with Helena Rubinstein, Arden invented the cosmetic industry as we know it today. In contrast to modern attitudes, wearing makeup in Arden's era was not only considered scandalous but an act of rebellious feminism.

Arden was a leading figure in the New York homosexual circle of the 1920s that included theater manager and politician Elizabeth Marbury; Mrs. William Vanderbilt; Marbury's lover, Elsie de Wolfe; and Anne Morgan.

8. EDNA ST. VINCENT MILLAY, 1892-1950, U.S.

Millay achieved fame at an early age. Although married to Eugen Boissevain, she was an ardent feminist and an outspoken advocate of sexual freedom, including bisexuality.

9. TALLULAH BANKHEAD, b. 1903, U.S.

One of the "four horsemen of the Algonquin" in 1920s New York, this film goddess was as outrageous for her bar-room wit as her sexual exploits.

Capote's *Answered Prayers* details a party at which actor Montgomery Clift arrived drunk and soon passed out. Dorothy Parker immediately commented on his beauty, saying it was a pity he was a "cocksucker."

Bankhead, in her typical stuttering style, replied "Well, d-d-dahling, I r-r-really wouldn't know. He's never sucked *my* cock."

10. NINA DYER, twentieth century, England

Married to both Baron Hans Heinrich Thyssen-Bornemisza and Prince Sadruddin Aga Khan, Dyer was "Oliver" to her women lovers. One of her lovers gave her a Cartier bracelet with the inscription "To my panther, untamed by man." She was, however, tamed by society and guilt-ridden by what she considered unnatural desires, and committed suicide in her late thirties.

11. JANE BOWLES, 1917-1973, U.S.

A novelist herself, Bowles was married to the author Paul Bowles, and spent much of her life living in Mexico, Spain, France, and Morocco. Considered to be one of the finest modern writers, her reputation rests solely on one novel, one play, and a handful of short stories. She is said to have died from the effects of "witchcraft" and alcohol during a fast for Ramadan.

12. FRIDA KAHLO, b. 1910, Mexico

An important surrealist painter, Kahlo had a stormy marriage to painter Diego Rivera that included affairs with women. Many of Kahlo's paintings reflect her feminist worldview.

13. BILLIE HOLIDAY, 1915-1959, U.S.

Though basically heterosexual, in her autobiography, *Lady Sings the Blues*, Holiday describes her lesbian experiences in prison, where a lesbian matron helped her survive the prison pecking order. Holiday also talks about a close relationship with a wealthy white lesbian in her life.

14. KATE MILLETT, b. 1934, U.S.

A noted feminist theorist who wrote *Sexual Politics*, one of the most influential books of the early 1970s, Millett described her affair with a woman in the autobiographical novel *Sita*. She talks about lesbianism and its political implications in her other books, including the book *Flying*.

5 Lesbians Who Married Gay Men

1. CARSON McCULLERS, 1917-1967, American novelist
Carson McCullers had a tempestuous relationship with Reeves McCullers; she married him in 1937 at an early age, divorced him a few years later, and married him again a few years after that. The first breakup came when she discovered they were both in love with the same man.

But jealousy over lovers wasn't their only problem. Reeves was obsessed with Carson's growing acclaim as a writer and with his own homosexuality. At one point, he threatened to kill them both. Carson was able to escape and left him; he committed suicide a short time later.

Known for novels about outsiders, Carson herself publicly admitted having at least one lesbian affair. She was also close friends with lesbian writers Elizabeth Bowen and Edith Sitwell.

2. VITA SACKVILLE-WEST, b. 1892, English author
Vita Sackville-West married Harold Nicolson while in her early twenties. Although they produced two children, were devoted friends throughout their lives, and never divorced, the marriage as such was short-lived.

3. BRYHER, 1894-1983, English novelist
Although she was already living with the poet H.D., who was nearly a decade older, Bryher asked writer Robert McAlmon to marry her when her wealthy family tried to force her to return home to be a proper British lady. As McAlmon was also gay, living with him gave them both a cover. Bryher gave him an allowance and he visited her parents to put on a show of respectability.

Using Bryher's money, McAlmon founded Contact Editions which published Bryher's lover, H.D., as well as Gertrude Stein and Hemingway.

"Bryher" is the pen name of Winifred Ellerman.

4. KATHARINE CORNELL, 1893-1974, German-American actress
Married to Broadway producer and director Guthrie McClintic,

this "First Lady of the American Theater" quietly had her own female attachments with women such as Eugenie Leontovich, who starred in the Broadway version of *Grand Hotel*, while McClintic had his own boyfriends.

5. ROMAINE BROOKS, 1874-1970, American-French painter

Romaine Goddard married John Ellingham Brooks at an early age but cut off her hair, donned male attire, and left him soon thereafter. Being possessed of a small fortune, she gave him an annuity upon divorce.

3 Native-American Berdache *

Cross-dressing has a long tradition among many Native-American tribes, with little of the taboo attached to it that exists in other cultures.

Generally, the individual adopted the identity of the opposite sex after having a dream in which he or she became the opposite sex. Many of these *berdache* became shamans and healers. Since they were thought to have magical powers and dealt with matters of life and death, they were often held in awe.

Most written records of berdache are from nineteenth-century explorers or early twentieth-century ethnographers.

1. KAÚXUMA NÚPIKA, nineteenth century, Kutenai

Qúqunok patke, "Mary White Pete," changed her name to Kaúxuma núpika, "Gone to the Spirits," after a dream in which the spirits changed her sex and gave her spiritual power. After the dream, she began to wear men's leggings, shirt, and breech cloth. She also began to carry a gun.

During her life, she married two women, led military campaigns, and helped negotiate a Flathead-Blackfoot peace treaty.

2. SAHAYKWISA, nineteenth century, Mojave

Sahaykwisá was not as lucky in life or love as Kaúxuma núpika. As both farmer and hunter she was a good provider but she was subjected to ridicule because she tended to brag about her life. One wife left her only to return, saying that Sahaykwisá was more satisfying than the woman's husband.

She was also a healer, and was reputed to be a witch who cast a spell on a man who spurned her advances.

3. *CÓ PAK*, early twentieth century, Klamath

Although Có pak kept female dress, she referred to herself as a man and is reported to have talked like one. She also married and, upon her wife's death some years later, wore a black belt, the sign of mourning men wore for their wives.

---

*The information in this list comes from *Gay American History*, by Jonathan Katz.

20 Native-American Tribes
with Women Berdache *

1. ATSUGEWI

2. BLACKFEET

3. COCOPA

4. DAKOTA

5. FLATHEAD

6. ILLINOIS

7. INGALIK

8. KLAMATH

9. KUTENAI

10. MARICOPA

11. MOJAVE

12. NAVAJO

13. NORTHERN PAIUTE

14. OJIBWA

15. QUINAULT

16. SANPOIL

17. SHOSHONI

18. YUKI

19. YUMA

20. ZUNI

*This information is taken from *Living the Spirit*, compiled by Will Roscoe and the Gay American Indian History Project.

20 Women Who Passed as Men

Until the nineteenth century, women's occupations were severely restricted. A single woman's options were often limited to being a governess, servant, or prostitute. Being able to pass as a man opened up her choices considerably. Even in the twentieth century, women have passed as men to get into male-dominated fields.

While not all such women were lesbians, the rise of cross-dressing and female transvestism in seventeenth- and eighteenth-century Europe was a way for women who loved other women to have lesbian relationships. Heterosexuality was such a dominant force that the only way lesbians could see themselves with other women was by adopting a complete change of attitude. If a woman loved another woman, the thinking went, then she must have been a man born in a woman's body.

1. DOÑA CATALINA DE ERAUZO, b. 1592, Spain

A soldier of fortune, Erauzo was called the Robin Hood of Latin America because she spent fifteen years in South America robbing the rich and helping the poor. Although Erauzo never married, she was engaged a number of times and passed as a man until she needed major surgery after being wounded. She then revealed her true sex.

But she was so famous by then that even pretending she was a man didn't matter. When she returned to her native Europe, she was celebrated as a hero. She continued to wear male attire and to pass as a man for the rest of her life.

2. CHRISTOPHER WELSH, late seventeenth century, England

On her husband's disappearance, Welsh began wearing male attire and ended up serving with Marlborough's forces, who defeated the French at Blenheim in 1704.

3. ROBERT SHURTLIEFF, b. 1760, U.S.

Deborah Sampson started her extraordinary career by being excommunicated from the First Baptist Church in Middleborough,

Massachusetts, after passing herself off as "Timothy Thayer," getting roaring drunk, and taking a black woman to bed.

As Shurtlieff, she joined the Continental Army where she became a Revolutionary War hero. She was granted a soldier's pension for her bravery and exemplary service.

In later life, she married and had two children.

4. HANNAH SNELL, b. 1723, England

Like many female transvestites, Snell began as a sailor but eventually put her experience to good use on the stage as a male impersonator, "Bill Bobstay the Sailor."

She died insane at Bedlam Hospital.

5. JAMES JOHN TAYLOR, b. 1778, England

Called "The British Amazon," Mary Anne Talbot spent many years at sea disguised as a man. She remained in drag even after legal threats.

6. CAPTAIN TWEED, nineteenth century, U.S.

Working her way up the ranks, Captain Tweed eventually commanded a trans-Atlantic ship.

7. ALEXANDER VASILEVICH, fl. 1829, Russia

Upon dressing in a Cossack uniform and fleeing her family, Nadezhda Durova changed her name to Vasilevich and joined the hussars. For ten years she passed as a man and was awarded the Cross of St. George for her exceptional bravery in that role.

Although she flirted with women, rumor finally caught up with her and she was called to St. Petersburg to explain herself to Tsar Alexander. While not exactly confessing, she begged not to be sent home; the tsar, considering her bravery, enrolled her in the Mariupol Hussars, one of Russia's best regiments. Vasilevich later achieved literary fame by writing an autobiography entitled *The Cavalry Maiden*, about her exploits.

8. CHARLEY WILSON, b. 1834, England

Catherine Coombs lived as a man for much of her life; she and her niece passed as man and wife for almost a decade. At age sixty-three, however, broke and penniless, Charley turned herself in to the poorhouse where she was forced to wear a dress and shawl, much against her will.

9. FRANKLIN THOMPSON, b. 1841, U.S.

Sarah Edmonds Seelye dressed as a man and called herself Franklin until she joined the Union Army. In an incredible double-reversal, she donned *women's* clothing to serve as a spy behind Confederate lines.

She later attended Oberlin College — in women's clothes — and published a book, *Nurse and Spy in the Union Army*, about her very complicated life.

10. KATHERINE VOSBAUGH, b. 1827, France

Vosbaugh donned men's clothes and shipped off to the Wild West where she began calling herself "Frenchy." She worked as a clerk, cook, bookkeeper, and shepherd — and she married another woman. Her sex wasn't discovered until she was brought to the hospital with pneumonia.

Even though everyone knew she was a woman, Vosburgh refused to return to women's dress and continued to wear men's clothing until her death two years later. At the hospital, she became known as "Grandpa."

11. CHARLES WINSLOW HALL, fl. 1901, U.S.

Caroline Hall decided to live her life as a man after "brooding over the disadvantages of being a woman," the Italian woman who later married her said. Hall died at age thirty-nine of consumption.

12. CHARLEY PARKHURST, 1812-1879, U.S.

A stagecoach driver, Charlotte Parkhurst was known to have shot and killed at least one bandit during her California gold-rush days.

13. JACK "BABE BEAN" GARLAND, b. 1869, U.S.

Born Elvira Virginia Mugarrieta to a prominent San Francisco family, Garland's father was the first Mexican consul to that city and her mother was the daughter of a Louisiana Supreme Court judge. Garland began wearing male attire to work as a reporter. She was picked up by the police, but knowing her rights, argued that there was nothing against women wearing men's clothes in the law — as long as there was no fraud involved. Garland was well liked and respected in her day. To see the Spanish-American War first-hand, she stowed away on an Army transport to the Philippines. She was also made an honorary member of the Stockton, California, Bachelor's Club.

14. PETER STRATFORD, d. 1929, New Zealand and U.S.

As Peter Stratford, Derestey Morton immigrated to America in 1904 and later married the screenwriter Beth Rouland.

15. GEORGE GREENE, nineteenth century, U.S.

At forty years of age, this Virginia woman married another woman and wasn't discovered to be a man until her death thirty-five years later. Her case was reported in a 1902 medical journal.

16. WILLIAM C. HOWARD, nineteenth century, U.S.

Howard lived her life as a happily married man and succeeded so well at her masquerade that the couple was able to adopt two children. Howard's case was also reported in an early twentieth-century medical journal.

17. MURRAY HALL, d. 1901, U.S.

Like William Howard, Murray Hall was so successful at passing that her adopted daughter didn't know her father was a woman until breast cancer hit at seventy years of age.

A part of the Tammany Hall political machine, Hall played the part to the hilt — drinking whiskey, smoking cigars, and playing poker. Her first wife left her for flirting with other women.

18. HARRY GORMAN, fl. 1903, U.S.

A railroad worker, Gorman passed as a man until she was discovered in a hospital at age forty. She claimed to know, on the New York Central Railway alone, at least ten other women who passed as men.

19. NICHOLAS DE RAYLAN, d. 1906, U.S.

As a man, this woman fought in the Spanish-American War

and worked as a secretary to the Russian consul. She had not one, but two wives; the first divorced her for her flings with chorus girls.

On her death of tuberculosis at age thirty-three, she was discovered to have an "elaborately-constructed artificial penis."

20. BILLY TIPTON, d. 1989, U.S.

On Tipton's death, her wife speculated that Tipton began to pass as a man because it was the only way she could play an instrument during the Big Band era. At the time, women were only allowed to sing and Tipton wanted to play the piano and saxophone. By living as a man, Tipton was able to spend her whole life as a musician, eventually having her own trio.

She was only discovered on her death. Her adopted sons knew nothing about her secret existence.

"I saw war, and I lived it, just as the soldier sees it and lives it, and for what I saw and learned I do not feel I paid too much."
—Elvira Mugarrieta, alias Jack "Babe Bean" Garland, cross-dressing reporter in the early twentieth century

13 Women Who Passed as Men — Until They Got Caught

1. POPE JOHN VIII, d. 858

According to a legend which persists today, there was not only a woman who passed herself off as a monk but who was so successful at the impersonation that she actually got herself elected to the office of pope. According to the story, "Pope Joan" was a scholar of note who initially dressed in men's attire to study philosophy. She became a cardinal under Pope Leo IV and was chosen for his office when he died. She fulfilled her duties faithfully and was not discovered until she became pregnant and gave birth. She was stoned to death by the enraged population immediately thereafter.

In 1601, Pope Clement VIII tried to put an end to the legend by declaring the story a myth and "Pope Joan" was removed from the official history of the Catholic Church. The historian Gibbon later ferreted out the actual person involved — a woman named Marozia who was so powerful that she got her son by Pope Sergius chosen as pope. Not only did her son hold the post but so did her grandson and great-grandson. For a woman who wanted to turn the papacy into a hereditary monarchy, she did pretty well.

The fact that she controlled the position for a number of years probably led to the mythical story of a cross-dressing female pope. Although she didn't actually hold that office, she did "wear the pants in the family" in this particular instance.

2. GEORGE HAMILTON, fl. 1746, England

An English doctor, Mary "Molly" Hamilton married women on three occasions. Each time she was eventually discovered and punished by flogging and imprisonment. Novelist Henry Fielding, who was also a judge, wrote about her case in the 1746 book, *The Female Husband*.

3. JOSEPH LOBDELL, b. 1829, U.S.

Lucy Ann Lobdell dressed as a man, became a hunter, and

eventually wed another woman; she described her experiences in her autobiography, *The Female Hunter of Delaware and Sullivan Counties*. Lobdell was eventually declared insane and died in a mental hospital.

4. JOHN WILKINSON, fl. 1907, U.S.

As a sailor with little privacy, Wilkinson was discovered to be a woman while bathing.

5. JAMES HOW, fl. 1750, England

Mary East donned men's clothes early in life to marry a childhood girlfriend. The two women lived together and ran a pub for over thirty years. During this time, someone who knew the secret began to blackmail her. She paid the blackmailer off for many years but finally turned to a local official in hopes of being protected. Her revelation brought surprise and consternation but because she was a prominent member of the community and had served in various parish offices, she was not arrested. The blackmailer was imprisoned, but as a result of the exposure and public scrutiny, Mary gave up the pub and went into retirement.

6. FRANK BLUNT, fl. 1894, U.S.

Anna Morris wore masculine attire nearly all her life and eventually married Gertrude Field. Little is known of her except that she was arrested in Wisconsin for theft, was discovered to be a woman, and received a sentence of one year in prison.

7. MILTON MATSON, fl. 1895, U.S.

Milton Matson was known as an English "swell" who was arrested in Los Gatos, California, for forging checks — to himself, in his real name, Luisa B. Matson.

8. RALPH KERWINIEO, fl. 1914, U.S.

As a man, Cora Anderson married twice, once to Dorothy Klenowski and another time to Marie White. Eventually a jilted girlfriend exposed her, and she was forced by the courts to go back to women's clothing.

9. EDWARD DE LACY EVANS, late nineteenth century, U.S.

Evans played the part of a man successfully until her discovery in 1879. Prior to the scandal the exposure caused, Evans had married three women: Marry Ann Delahunty, Sarah Moore, and Julia Marquand.

10. JOHANN BURGER, fl. 1908, U.S.

Burger was arrested in St. Louis for male impersonation and kidnapping a woman she had managed to marry.

11. COL. SIR VICTOR BARKER, fl. 1929, England

An Army officer who married a woman, Lillian Arkel Smith was discovered and sentenced to nine months' imprisonment for entering a false statement in a marriage register.

12. JAMES "JOHN" HATHAWAY, b. 1829, U.S.

During her lifetime, Ethel Kimball was arrested for forgery, for passing herself off as a wealthy man, and for marrying Louise M. Achtler after a two-year courtship. She ended up pleading guilty to "falsifying the record" when she unsuccessfully applied for the marriage license as a man.

13. JIM McHARRIS, fl. 1940, U.S.

A black woman, Annie Lee Grant lived as a man and worked as a short-order cook, gas station attendant, and preacher from the late 1930s to the early 1950s, when she was arrested for a traffic ticket and was discovered to be a woman in male attire.

"The thing of being skewed up in tight pants and subject to the flapping of petticoats is to me unbearable."
—Luisa Matson, who passed as
Milton Matson for most of her life

10 European Cross-Dressing Women Who Had Their Autobiographies Published*

1. MARIA VAN ANTWERPEN, Dutch, 1751
   De Bredasche Heldinne
2. RENÉE BORDEREAU, French, 1814
   Memoires de Renée Bordereau, dite Langevin, traitant sa vie militaire dans la Vendée
3. CHRISTIAN DAVIES, English, 1740
   The Life and Adventures of Mrs. Christian Davies commonly called Mother Ross, who, in several campaigns under King William and the late Duke of Marlborough in the quality of a foot soldier and dragoon gave many signal proofs of an unparallell'd courage and personal bravery, Taken from her own mouth when a pensioner of Chelsea-Hospital
4. FRANÇOISE DESPRÈS, French, 1817
   Details historiques sur les services de Françoise Desprès, employée dans les armées royales de la Vendée depuis 1773 jusqu'en 1815...
5. MARY FRITH, English, 1662
   The life and death of Mrs. M.F., commonly called Mol Cut- purse
6. MARIA TER MEETELEN, Dutch, 1743
   De vrouwelyke soldaat
7. JEAN DE PRÉCHAC, French, 1713
   L'Heroine mousquetaire, histoire veritable
8. HANNAH SNELL, English, 1750
   The Female Soldier; or the Surprising Life and Adventures of Hannah Snell
9. MARY ANNE TALBOT, English, 1809
   The Life and Surprising Adventures of Mary Anne Talbot in the Name of John Taylor, a Natural Daughter of the Late Earl Talbot...
10. ANNE JANE THORNTON, English, 1835
    Interesting Life and Wonderful Adventures of A.J. Thornton, the Female Soldier...

*From *The Tradition of Female Transvestism in Early Modern Europe*, by Rudolf M. Dekker and Lotte C. van de Pol.

2 Black Women Who Cross-Dressed*

Prior to the Civil War, many black women who weren't gay dressed as men to escape slavery.

1. ELLEN CRAFT

In 1848, Ellen persuaded her husband William to try a brilliant escape. Being light-skinned, Ellen would play the master while William acted the slave. Dressed in top hat, beard, and glasses, Ellen pretended she was a young man.

The bold idea worked. Traveling first class by ship and train, they got to Philadelphia on Christmas Day that year.

2. MARIA WEEMS

At a young age, this daring black woman disguised herself as a boy and by sheer cunning was able to escape her master and take the Underground Railroad to freedom.

*This information came from *We Are Your Sisters*, edited by Dorothy Sterling.

17 Women Who Wore Men's Clothing

Throughout the centuries, women have assumed the symbols of male power. By adopting male clothing, they were able to further careers in ways impossible had they stayed in female dress. Many of these women took on other "male" attributes, including the love of women.

1. HATSHEPSUT, reigned about 1503-1482 B.C., Egypt
The wife of Thutmose, Hatshepsut ruled Egypt for nearly twenty years following her husband's death. She took the title of Pharaoh, wore royal masculine dress and a beard which signified kingship, and led the Egyptian army into battle.

While it was not uncommon for a widow to assume the king's role until the male heir was old enough to reign, Hatshepsut ruled until long after the official heir was of age.

2. JEANNE D'ARC, 1412-1431, France
After a number of visions in which she saw saints who commanded her to wear men's clothing and drive the English out of France, Jeanne d'Arc obtained permission to dress as a man and was made a captain in the Army. Her leadership was responsible for the siege of Orleans, which gave Charles VII victory over the English forces. Jeanne was later captured by the English, who accused her of witchcraft and heresy. She was burned as a heretic in 1431 and canonized as a saint in 1920.

3. LOUISE LABÉ, about 1524-1566, near France
This famous lesbian poet so excelled at horsemanship that she participated in a tournament at Lyon in 1542 — an event so unusual that it developed into a legend that she had participated in a siege.

4. MARY FRITH, 1584-1659, England
A ruffian and thief known as "Moll — or Mal — Cutpurse," Frith dressed as a man whenever it best suited her needs. Undeterred by the usual confines of her sex, she was a highwayman who became quite rich by leading her own band of robbers. She

became a legend who eventually settled down to open up a "pawn" shop where people who'd been robbed could retrieve their stolen goods. The play *The Roaring Girl, or Moll Cutpurse* was a tremendous success on the stage during her life and her posthumously published autobiography a great success after.

5. ANNE BONNEY, fl. about 1718, Ireland, and MARY READ, b. 1690, England

These two women pirates are perhaps the most illustrious cross-dressers in history. They each married men a number of times, including one "Calico Jack" who had himself been a captain's paramour. As a working threesome, they made a formidable team, roaming the high seas in search of ships full of loot. During their career they stole a number of ships, the most famous of which was *The Royal Queen*. Bonney and Read were eventually caught and convicted in 1720. Ever resourceful, Bonney pleaded pregnancy to get off the hook and Read also managed a reprieve. The rest of the crew were hanged. They were most likely lovers, with Mary sometimes passing as "Mark."

6. LADY HESTER STANHOPE, b. 1776, England

Stanhope was an aristocrat who left the cozy confines of Britain to roam the world in men's clothes. She eventually settled in the North African desert and bought a monastery with her lover, Elizabeth Williams.

Later in life, her eccentricity seems to have gotten the better of her. When her annual government pension was stopped, she walled herself into her monastic retreat and died penniless.

7. ROSA BONHEUR, 1822-1899, France

The famed painter of landscapes and animals, Rosa Bonheur was issued a permit to dress as a man — ostensibly to give her more freedom to pursue a career that entailed visiting slaughterhouses to study animal anatomy.

8. GEORGE SAND, 1804-1876, France

George Sand was as famous in her day for her eccentric habits — which included cross-dressing, smoking cigars, and chasing women — as for her writing.

9. LYDIA ANN PUYFER, fl. 1854, U.S.

Like so many others, Puyfer was lured to the West by the California Gold Rush — only Puyfer left in her male cousin's clothes and never went back to the East or to female clothing.

10. MARY EDMONIA LEWIS, 1843-1909, U.S.

A black woman artist and member of actress Charlotte Cushman's "Jolly Bachelors," Lewis chose to wear masculine attire at a time when women were particularly oppressed by bulky, cumbersome female clothes.

11. HARRIET HOSMER, b. 1830, U.S.

Hosmer, too, was part of Charlotte Cushman's circle and joined Cushman on her rides through the streets of Rome — both dressed in male attire.

12. MME. JEANNE DIEULAFOY, 1851-1916, France

An archaeologist, Madame Dieulafoy discovered the Temple of Darius and was given the Order of the Legion of Honor by the French government. She was also given permission to wear men's attire at all times.

13. CALAMITY JANE, c. 1852-1903, U.S.

One of the most famous Wild West scouts, Calamity Jane was also miner, hunter, and trapper who rarely wore women's clothes. A woman of the hardiest sort, she outlived a number of husbands — including Wild Bill Hickok — and didn't take any guff from anyone. Lightning-fast with a gun in an era when quick-draw artists were the norm, she was known to be especially "quick to avenge any insult to her sex."

14. MARY FIELDS, b. about 1832, U.S.

Fields, a former slave who settled in the West to make a name for herself as "Stagecoach Mary," never married and rarely wore women's dress. Like so many other cross-dressing women of her day, she was known to be partial to cigars.

15. AMELIA EARHART, 1897-1937, U.S.

The first woman to fly solo over the Atlantic, Earhart was also the first person to fly from Hawaii to California. During her short life, she founded a women's flying group and advised women students at Purdue University on careers.

In an era when women were still confined to dresses, Earhart wore her aviator clothing in the air and on the ground. She disappeared in 1937 while flying over the Pacific Ocean.

Today there is almost as much speculation surrounding Earhart's sexuality as there is her death. Before marrying George Putnam, she wrote to him that she would not hold him to any medieval conception of faithfulness nor would she consider herself bound by one. She was also reluctant to marry for fear that it would get in the way of her career.

16. ZORA NEALE HURSTON, 1891-1960, U.S.

Hurston was a black American novelist who wrote *Their Eyes Were Watching God*, and wore pants and rakish hats. She smoked cigars at a time when few women even smoked cigarettes.

17. HANNAH "GLUCK" GLUCKSTEIN, b. 1895, England

Born into a family that founded a wealthy British catering firm, Gluckstein rejected the expectations of her upbringing and class, and instead became an artist. She was so successful that her exhibitions in the 1920s and 1930s drew such notables as Queen Mary and Cecil Beaton.

Despite a bohemian lifestyle that included affairs with society women, she never quite gave up her background. She wore men's clothes but the designs were by Victor Steibel and Elsa Schiaparelli.

"I was … so certain of my self-respect that I never viewed it from a conventional standpoint."
—Sarah Seelye, who passed as Civil War soldier Franklin Thompson

18 Actresses Who Appeared in Drag

1. HANNAH SNELL, British stage

2. KATE CARNEY, British music hall

3. LIL HAWTHORNE, British music hall

4. GERTRUDE LAWRENCE, British music hall

5. VESTA TILLEY, British music hall

6. GLADYS FERGUSSON, American stage

7. EDITH STOREY, *A Florida Enchantment*

8. SANDRA SHAW, *Blood Money*

9. MARIE PREVOST, *Yankee Doodle in Berlin*

10. MARLENE DIETRICH, *Morocco* and *Blonde Venus*

11. KATHARINE HEPBURN, *Sylvia Scarlett*

12. MARION DAVIES, *Beverly of Graustark*, *Marianne*, and *Little Old New York*

13. IRENE DUNNE, *My Favorite Wife*

14. MARY MARTIN, *Peter Pan*

15. LILY TOMLIN, *Performing Nightly* (as Rick, the singles-bar cruiser)

16. JULIE ANDREWS, *Victor/Victoria*

17. BARBRA STREISAND, *Yentl*

18. LINDA HUNT, *The Year of Living Dangerously*

16 Women
Who Wrote under Men's Names

The first female writer to make a living from her work, seventeenth-century Aphra Behn, had no need to disguise her sex. But by the nineteenth century, women writers had to pretend to be men in order to be taken seriously.

1. MARY ANNE EVANS, "George Eliot"

Toasted by Turgenev as the greatest living novelist, this nineteenth-century Englishwoman wrote *The Mill on the Floss, Middlemarch, Adam Bede*, and many other novels, under the pseudonym "George Eliot." Together with the Brontës and Jane Austen, Eliot brought the art of the novel to new heights.

2. CHARLOTTE BRONTË, "Currer Bell," 1816-1855

Author of the immediate sensation *Jane Eyre*, which still holds its own today, Charlotte wrote under a pseudonym at first.

3. EMILY BRONTË, "Ellis Bell," 1818-1848

Nineteenth-century English author of the masterpiece *Wuthering Heights*, Brontë was one of three sisters who felt they had to disguise their sex to be accepted as authors.

4. ANNE BRONTË, "Acton Bell," 1820-1849

Anne and her two sisters published their first volume of verse under the title *Poems by Currer, Ellis and Acton Bell*.

5. AMANDINE AURORE LUCIE DUPIN, THE BARONNE DUDEVANT, "George Sand"

Sand was the author of many widely-read nineteenth-century French novels, including *Indiana* and *Valentine*. It was her *Lélia* which with its fierce eroticism caused the most scandal.

6. & 7. KATHERINE "Michael" BRADLEY and EDITH "Henry" COOPER, "Michael Field"

This aunt and niece who lived together for many years made a living by writing poems and plays under the male pseudonym "Michael Field." When it was discovered some years later that the duo was not a man but two women, their work fell out of favor.

8. VIOLET PAGET, "Vernon Lee," b. 1856

Born in France, Paget wrote many books set in Italy, where she spent most of her life.

9. VIOLET FLORENCE MARTIN, "Martin Ross"

Part of the duo of "Somerville and Ross," these two women, who worked and lived together for much of their lives, wrote *An Irish Cousin*, and other works, in early twentieth-century Ireland.

10. BARONESS KAREN BLIXEN, "Isak Dinesen," 1885-1962

The early twentieth-century Danish author of *Seven Gothic Tales*, *Winter Tales*, and *Out of Africa* wrote under the Dinesen pseudonym and also published *Angelic Avengers*, about the Nazi occupation, under the name "Pierre Andrezel."

11. MRS. GUY BOLTON, "Stephen Powys"

Bolton wrote the lesbian drama *Wise Tomorrow*, which debuted on Broadway in 1937 under a man's name, safely hiding her identity.

12. ETHEL FLORENCE ROBERTSON, "Henry Handel Richardson," 1870-1946

Robertson was an early twentieth-century Australian novelist who wrote *Maurice Guest* in 1908. It was the first novel published in Britain to treat homosexuality honestly and openly.

13. FLORENCE MARGARET SMITH, "Stevie Smith"

A twentieth-century British poet who never married, Smith called herself "Stevie" in print. Her career spanned many decades during which she wrote many volumes of poetry, including *A Good Time was Had by All* in 1937 and *Not Waving But Drowning* in 1957.

14. OLIVE SCHREINER, "Ralph Iron," 1855-1920

Schreiner, a suffragist, wrote under the pseudonym "Ralph Iron" for many years before revealing her true name and sex. She called herself an "invert," the term for lesbianism in the early twentieth century, and is believed to have had a lengthy affair with Dr. Havelock Ellis, who tried to convince her that she was heterosexual. She eventually married, but wasn't happy in that role. She is best known today for *The Story of an African Farm.*

15. HELEN DINER, "Sir Galahad," 1874-1948

The German author of the feminist classic, *Mothers and Amazons,* Diner also wrote under a protective male pseudonym during the early years of her literary career. Her 1938 book *Imperial Byzantium* was published under this name. Diner was born Bertha Ekstein-Diener.

16. PATRICIA STONEHOUSE, "Harlingham Quinn"

A number of Australian women writers have worked under men's names during their careers and Stonehouse was no exception. She used a number of pen names during her long career.

Lesbians and the Law

12 Political Activists
Who Had Romantic Friends or Lovers

1. SUSAN B. ANTHONY, b. 1820, U.S.

One of America's most renowned feminists, Anthony founded the National Women's Suffrage Association with her lifelong friend and political comrade, Elizabeth Cady Stanton.

Anthony decided to remain a "spinster" early in life, to free herself from male bondage and devote her time to the feminist cause. Although only fragments of correspondence remain, Anthony's ardent letters to Anna Dickinson, known as the "Queen of the Lyceum" for her superstar orator status, hardly sound like the stereotype of a screeching suffragist with the "My Dear Chicky Dicky Darling" salutation. Anthony had a close relationship with Dickinson for many years but Dickinson finally broke it off.

Anthony's closest friend all of her life was Elizabeth Cady Stanton. She said of Stanton: "In our friendship of years there has never been the break of one hour ... So closely interwoven have been our lives, our purposes, and experiences that separated, we have a feeling of incompleteness."

Although they did not live together, Anthony spent the last four years of her life with another friend, Anna Howard Shaw.

2. HARRIET MARTINEAU, 1802-1876, England

A vivid feminist and abolitionist whose writings covered a wide range of social issues, Martineau supported herself by writing articles for the general populace on such topics as economics and political issues of the day. She worked as a journalist for the *London Daily News* and also wrote children's stories.

Martineau was closely connected with American educator Margaret Fuller.

3. FRANCES WILLARD, 1839-1898, U.S.

The head of the Women's Christian Temperance Union — one of the strongest feminist organizations of its day — Willard also claimed in her autobiography that she had over fifty "heart affairs" with both women and men. One important relationship was with

Kate A. Jackson, who followed Willard to Genesee Wesleyan Seminary and Northwestern University to be near her.

Willard was also involved for twelve years with Anna A. Gordon, whom she called "Little Heart's-ease."

4. LOUISE MICHEL, 1830-1905, France

A socialist and revolutionary, Michel participated in the 1871 Paris Commune, and was among its last defenders at Père Lachaise cemetery. She was sentenced to life imprisonment but was released in the 1880 amnesty.

Upon her release, she returned to active politics and was again arrested for leading strikes. This time she fled to the safety of London — where she lived with Charlotte Vauvalle.

5. LUCY STONE, 1818-1893, U.S.

Stone, an American feminist and abolitionist, has been linked closely with her sister-in-law, political activist Antoinette Brown Blackwell. Both women were married but their correspondence includes such endearments as "My Little Cowboy."

6. JANE ADDAMS, 1860-1935, U.S.

The founder of Hull House, Addams campaigned for the rights of women and the poor all her life. She helped found the American Civil Liberties Union (ACLU) and won a Nobel Peace Prize for her tireless work in 1931.

In addition to her political activities, Addams spent forty years with Mary Rozet Smith. She founded Hull House with another companion, Ellen Gates Starr. Addams was also part of a close female support network with such other activist-suffragists as Alice Hamilton, who worked with Addams at Hull House for over twenty years.

7. LILLIAN WALD, b. 1867, U.S.

Wald almost single-handedly created the nursing profession as we know it today — without religious affiliation and done for the public health. She also founded the Henry Street Settlement, an all-women nursing institution, in one of Manhattan's worst slums.

A friend of Jane Addams, Wald was president of the American Union Against Militancy — a pacifist organization that tried to keep the U.S. out of World War I and later evolved into the ACLU.

Wald had many romantic friendships during her long "single" life — from the women she worked with at Henry Street to society ladies such as Park Avenue socialite Mabel Hyde Kittredge and New York Judge Helen Arthur.

Like Addams, Wald had an extensive female support network. Some of the women who lived at Henry Street and called themselves her "steadies" had friendships that lasted over fifty years. These women included Helene MacDowell, Lavinia L. Dock (known as "Docky"), Anne Goodrich, Ysabella Waters, and Florence Kelley (who was also close friends with Addams).

In addition to living and working together at Henry Street, the women often vacationed together in Mexico, the West Indies, and Japan with the women from Hull House.

8. MARY GREW, b. 1813, U.S.

An abolitionist and feminist, Grew was the lifelong companion of Margaret Burleigh.

9. MIRIAM DANIELLE, nineteenth century, England

Danielle, a feminist and socialist, immigrated to America with her political comrade of many years, Helena Born.

10. MARGARET ANDERSON, early twentieth century, U.S.

Best known as the editor of the literary magazine *The Little Review*, Anderson was also an activist who used her magazine to publish one of the earliest militant defenses of homosexuality in the U.S.

11. ELIZABETH MARBURY, early twentieth century, U.S.

A society woman who was politically active on progressive issues such as feminism, Marbury was married but carried on a known liaison with actress and interior decorator Elsie de Wolfe.

12. BARBARA DEMING, twentieth century, U.S.

Deming's career spans the issues of mid-twentieth-century America from civil rights to peace activism and the anti-war protests of the Vietnam era. Her book *We Are All Part of One Another* collects her essays. Her very autobiographical and very lesbian novel *A Humming Under My Feet* (published in the U.K. by The Women's Press) is one of the best-kept secrets in modern lesbian literature.

9 Turn-of-the-Century German Activists *

One of the first openly gay political movements started in turn-of-the-century Germany. Although men made up the initial group, women-identified women — many of whom had been romantic friends — soon joined their ranks.

Homosexuals in those days called themselves "uranians." By 1906, there were 1.2 million uranians in Germany; 56,000 in the city of Berlin. The movement continued to grow until Hitler began the homosexual pogroms that eventually exterminated thousands of gay men and lesbians.

1. ELISABETH DAUTHENDEY, novelist
Her 1900 book, *Of the New Woman and her Love*, argued for the romantic ideal of women-identified love being higher than a heterosexual union because it was spiritual rather than sexual.

2. AIMÉE DUC, novelist
Her book, *Are These Women?* (1903) answered "yes" and was one of the first lesbian novels with a happy ending.

3. MARIA JANITSCHEK, author
As early as 1906, her *The New Eve* argued that nurture, not nature, "caused" homosexuality.

4. E. KRAUSE, author
Little is known about Krause except that she wrote an essay called *The Truth About Me*, which appeared in the 1906 volume, *Yearbook of Intermediate Sexual Types*.

5. MARIE-MADELEINE, BARONESS VON PUTTKAMER, poet
Although Marie-Madeleine used the French decadent imagery such as crucifixions and death, her 1895 book of poetry, *Auf Kypros*, had poems to Sappho.

6. GABRIELLE REUTER, novelist
In the 1895 novel, *A Girl From a Nice Family*, Reuter traces the

changing mores of the time and the social stigma which was rapidly growing around female friendships. In 1921, Reuter also wrote an autobiographical novel entitled *From Childhood to Maturity*.

7. ANNA RUELING, activist and public speaker

Her 1904 speech, *What Interest Does the Woman's Movement Have in the Homosexual Question?* was one of the first to point out that lesbians often led the women's rights movement.

8. ROSA VON BRAUNSCHWEIG, author

Von Braunschweig was one of the first to argue that homosexuals were "born that way." She also wrote a 1903 biography of the lesbian opera diva Felicita von Vestvali.

9. ANNA WEIRAUCH, novelist

Although it contains one of the first scenes of lesbian lovemaking, Weirauch's 1919 three-volume novel *The Scorpion* reflects the emerging influence of the sexologists by treating romantic friendships and lesbianism as a sickness. In it, one character commits suicide and the other is forced to marry.

The novel was the prototype for most twentieth-century novels written about lesbianism until the emergence of lesbian-identified publishing houses of the 1970s.

*The material in this list comes from *Lesbian-Feminism in Turn-of-the-Century Germany*, by Lillian Faderman and Brigitte Eriksson.

"Other women will go on from here, others will succeed where I failed."

—Violette Leduc, lesbian novelist

10 Lesbians in the Fight against AIDS

In 1989, the total number of Americans to die of AIDS passed the number of Americans who died in combat in the Vietnam War.

Although lesbians have not been as drastically affected by AIDS as their gay male counterparts, the emotional cost has been great. Lesbians across the nation have risen to the challenge, donating endless amounts of time and money to the gay community in its hour of need. These are a few of those women.

1. CAITLAIN RYAN

Ryan co-authored *AIDS: A Public Health Challenge*, the first major review of state AIDS policy. The report was commissioned by the U.S. Public Health Service in 1986.

Two years later, as a result of her work in the field of AIDS health care, Ryan received the highest honor the field of social work gives its members — the National Social Worker of the Year award.

2. INES RIEDER

Rieder co-edited the book *AIDS: The Women*, which includes moving articles and personal stories about the toll AIDS is taking. Contributors include such lesbian authors as Louise Rafkin, Deborah Stone, Lea Sanchez, and Cherie Pies.

3. CARY NORSWORTHY

One of many women fighting the battle for AIDS services at the local level, Norsworthy ran the San Francisco AIDS Foundation Food Bank for five years.

4. SUZANN GAGE

Gage has been involved with feminist health care since the early 1970s. She is co-founder of the Women's AIDS Project in Los Angeles.

5. CAROL JONAS

An activist for nearly twenty years, Jonas is involved with

ACT-UP, the grass-roots political organization that is fighting the government's slow response to AIDS. The nationwide group is also trying to get a more positive response to AIDS — and to homosexuality in general — from the health and insurance industries.

6. ELIZABETH HARRISON

As president of the American Association of Physicians for Human Rights, Harrison has been lobbying the Food and Drug Administration for quicker testing of experimental drugs and access to experimental medication for people with life-threatening illnesses such as AIDS.

7. & 8. SHADOW MORTON and SKY RENFRO

Through their efforts, these two women raised eight thousand dollars for AIDS organizations in the first year of the Ms. Leather contest.

9. DIANNA GARCIA

Garcia has been in the fight against AIDS since 1985 when she started a local support group for people with AIDS. Since then, she has headed an AIDS-education program and created a bi-lingual hot line for AIDS information that is available in both Spanish and English.

10. VIRGINIA URIBE

The founder of Project 10, Uribe has been working for the past six years to get accurate AIDS information into the public schools. She does workshops for teachers about AIDS and about homophobic stereotypes which hinder the ability of gay teenagers to develop a positive sense of self.

14 Lesbians Who Were Elected or Appointed to Public Office

1. JUDY ABDO, elected to Santa Monica (California) City Council, November 8, 1988.

2. TAMMY BALDWIN, became member of the Dane County Board of Supervisors, Madison, Wisconsin, on April 15, 1986.

3. KAREN CLARK, elected state representative of Minnesota, November 1980.

4. SHARON DAY, appointed to the St. Paul Human (Minnesota) Rights Commission, January 8, 1987.

5. DARLENE GARNER, appointed acting director of the Mayor's Commission on Sexual Minorities, Philadelphia, May 1, 1987. Named executive director of the Commission, August 24, 1987.

6. LEE HUDSON, appointed liaison to the mayor, New York, December 12, 1983. Named director of the Mayor's Office for the Lesbian and Gay Community, March 20, 1989.

7. ANNE JENNINGS, became deputy attorney general, San Francisco, July 1979.

8. MARCY KAHN, appointed judge of the Criminal Court, New York, February 24, 1987.

9. KATHY KOZACHENKO, elected to the Ann Arbor (Michigan) City Council, April 1974.

10. JOAN LOBIS, elected Civil Court judge, New York, January 1, 1989.

11. BARBARA JEAN (BJ) METZGER, appointed to the St. Paul (Minnesota) Human Rights Commission, January 7, 1986.

12. MARY MORGAN, appointed Municipal Court judge, San Francisco, September 10, 1981.

13. KATHLEEN NICHOLS, became member of the Dane County Board of Supervisors, Madison, Wisconsin, April 20, 1982.

14. ELAINE VALADEZ, became member of the Minneapolis Civil Rights Commission, August 1986.

19 Lesbian Firsts

Because so much lesbian history is ignored and the contributors forgotten, each new generation feels it is reinventing the wheel. Thus, pinpointing lesbian "firsts" is difficult, and many entries on this list are only tentative.

1. FIRST USE OF THE WORD "LESBIAN" TO DENOTE A WOMAN-LOVING WOMAN — AS OPPOSED TO SOMEONE FROM THE ISLE OF LESBOS: In an article in the medical journal *The Alienist and Neurologist*, about lesbian cross-dresser Lucy Ann "Joseph" Lobdell, 1883.

2. FIRST USE OF THE WORD "LESBIAN" IN A NEWSPAPER ARTICLE: *New York Times* headline "Lesbian Love and Murder" about Alice Mitchell's murder of Freda Ward, 1892.

3. FIRST WOMAN DOCTOR IN ENGLAND: Lesbian James Miranda Barry, born 1795, who earned her medical degree from Edinburgh College while still in her teens and lived as a man all her life.

4. FIRST WOMAN DIVINITY STUDENT IN THE U.S.: Suffragist Antoinette Brown Blackwell, romantic friend and sister-in-law of Lucy Stone, graduated from Oberlin College, 1850.

5. FIRST WOMAN AWARDED THE BRITISH ORDER OF MERIT: Florence Nightingale, British nurse and administrator who, with the introduction of hygiene and modern standards of medicine, lowered the death rate in Crimean War hospitals from 42 percent to 2.2 percent. There is much speculation about Nightingale's life because she never married and had many close women friends. An excellent biography of her is included in Lytton Strachey's *Eminent Victorians*.

6. FIRST PLAY TO PORTRAY ACTRESSES KISSING AND HUGGING ON AN AMERICAN STAGE: *A Florida Enchantment*, at the Park Theatre in New York, 1896.

7. FIRST PUBLIC FIGURE TO SUPPORT GAY AND LESBIAN RIGHTS IN THE U.S.: Political activist Emma Goldman, ro-

mantic friend and possible lover of activist Almeda Sperry, began speaking publicly on the issue in 1910.

8. FIRST WRITTEN DEFENSE OF HOMOSEXUALITY IN THE U.S.: "Two Points of View," in Margaret Anderson's *Little Review*, 1913.

9. FIRST PLAY ABOUT LESBIANS WRITTEN BY AN AMERICAN: *Hymn to Venus*, by William Hurlbut, opened in New York in 1926.

10. FIRST AMERICAN LESBIAN PUBLICATION: *Vice Versa*, 1947.

11. FIRST OPENLY LESBIAN ORGANIZATION IN BRITAIN: The Minorities Research Group, 1964.

12. FIRST MAJOR FEMINIST ORGANIZATION TO IDENTIFY LESBIAN RIGHTS AS A NATIONAL PRIORITY: National Organization for Women, 1975.

13. FIRST OPEN LESBIAN TO BE ORDAINED A PRIEST: Episcopal minister, the Rev. Ellen Barrett, 1977.

14. FIRST LESBIANS TO DANCE OPENLY AT THE WHITE HOUSE: Barbara Love and Kay Whitlock, who waltzed to chamber music in the lobby, 1978.

15. FIRST OPENLY GAY STAND-UP COMIC ON TELEVISION: Robin Tyler, *First Annual Funny Women's Show*, 1978.

16. FIRST WOMAN NAMED TO THE ACADÉMIE FRANÇAISE: Lesbian novelist Marguérite Yourcenar, 1980.

17. FIRST WOMAN TO REACH THE NORTH POLE: Lesbian Ann Bancroft, 1986.

18. FIRST LESBIAN SORORITY: Lambda Delta Lambda, University of California, Los Angeles, 1988.

19. FIRST OPENLY LESBIAN POLITICAL REFUGEE TO ASK FOR U.S. ASYLUM AND CHALLENGE IMMIGRATION AND NATURALIZATION SERVICE: Masha Gessen, Jewish political refugee from the Soviet Union, who was granted citizenship in 1989.

6 Countries with the Harshest Penalties against Lesbianism *

1. CUBA: Maximum 20 years' imprisonment. In addition, parents are supposed to report any homosexual activity on the part of their children to the authorities.

2. TRINIDAD AND TOBAGO: 20 years' imprisonment.

3. PAKISTAN: 100 lashes — from which people have died.

4. LIBYA: Islamic law punishes homosexual acts by "throwing the performer of those acts down from the highest level."

5. IRAN: Death.

6. SAUDI ARABIA: Death.

*All information on international law in this section is taken from the International Lesbian and Gay Association's *Pink Book*, second edition, 1988.

"I prefer a tyrant of my own sex, so I shall not deny the patent fact of my subjection; for I do believe that I have developed into much more of a woman under her jurisdiction..."
— Elizabeth Cady Stanton of Susan B. Anthony

14 Countries with the Harshest Penalties against Male Homosexuality but No Laws against Lesbianism

Unfortunately, an absence of criminal penalties does not necessarily imply tolerance in a society. In India, where oral sex is illegal and male homosexual acts can result in a maximum of life imprisonment, two lesbian police officers used the absence of legal prohibitions to their advantage in 1987 to marry each other. But as a result they were fired from their jobs.

1. IRELAND

2. SOVIET UNION

3. BERMUDA

4. JAMAICA

5. KENYA

6. MOZAMBIQUE

7. NIGERIA

8. SOUTH AFRICA

9. TANZANIA

10. UGANDA

11. ZAMBIA

12. HONG KONG

13. SINGAPORE

14. INDIA

8 Countries Where the Age of Consent Is Higher for Homosexuals — and Two Interesting Exceptions

1. FINLAND: 18 years versus 16 years.

2. GERMAN DEMOCRATIC REPUBLIC: 18 years versus 14 years.

3. HUNGARY: 18 years versus 14 years.

4. LUXEMBOURG: 18 years versus 14 years.

5. SURINAME: 18 years versus 16 years.

6. SWITZERLAND: 20 years versus 16 years.

7. AUSTRIA: The age of consent is 14 years for lesbians and heterosexuals; 18 for male homosexuals.

8. GREECE: The age of consent is based on gender rather than sexual orientation — 17 years for men versus 16 for women.

5 of the Best Countries in Which to Live (from a Legal Standpoint) if You Are Lesbian

1. DENMARK

As of 1989, Denmark has allowed lesbians and gay men to marry. A historic bill which passed the Danish Parliament on May 27 would allow couples to marry in town halls and provide equal rights in housing, social welfare, and pensions. The only two drawbacks: gay couples could not marry in churches or adopt children.

Prior to the marriage law, an anti-discrimination law had been in effect since 1987. Even before that, lesbian couples could inherit property from each other.

Gays can also enlist in the military and be drafted.

2. FINLAND

Equal social benefits are recognized for gay partners although lesbians and gay men cannot yet marry. Anti-gay discrimination is still legal in jobs, adoption, and foster parenthood, and the penal code prohibits encouragement of homosexuality.

3. THE NETHERLANDS

In general, Dutch lesbians and gay men are protected against discrimination.

In 1987, the government broadened the definition of libel to include anti-gay remarks made in public. That year, the archbishop of Utrecht was sued for publicly siding with a landlord who had refused to rent a room to a homosexual. In that same year, a couple was sentenced to be fined 6,000 guilders each time they said that homosexuals caused AIDS.

Homosexuals also serve in the military, where they are protected from discrimination. The Dutch government has protested the U.S. military's policy of harassing gay American soldiers stationed in The Netherlands.

4. NORWAY

Anti-discrimination laws make it illegal to publicly threaten, insult, or bear hatred toward homosexuals. At least one evangelical minister has been fined for making anti-homosexual remarks on radio.

Gays are also allowed to serve in the military.

5. SWEDEN

In 1988, Sweden became the first country to allow homosexuals to marry. Even before that, it was a crime to make derogatory remarks about a person's homosexuality. It is also illegal for commercial establishments to discriminate against gays.

Gay couples who live together are protected under Swedish cohabitation laws, which give them the same rights as heterosexual couples who live together but aren't married.

School curriculums include unbiased information about homosexuality.

12 U.S. States Where Lesbian Acts Are Still Illegal*

Although sodomy is often perceived as an exclusively male act, every sodomy law in the U.S. today criminalizes sexual behavior between women as well as between men. The only distinction is that in some states oral sex is legal for heterosexuals but not for homosexuals.

1. IDAHO, 5 years minimum

2. NEVADA, 6 years for sodomy between homosexuals

3. DISTRICT OF COLUMBIA, 10 years

4. OKLAHOMA, 10 years

5. NORTH CAROLINA, 10 years

6. MONTANA, 10 years for sodomy between homosexuals

7. MISSISSIPPI, 10 years

8. MARYLAND, 10 years

9. TENNESSEE, 15 years

10. RHODE ISLAND, 20 years

11. GEORGIA, 20 years for sodomy between homosexuals

12. MICHIGAN, 15 years for first time; life for repeat offenders

*Courtesy of the National Gay and Lesbian Task Force Privacy Project.

10 Laws and Significant Omissions

1. PRE-COLUMBIAN MEXICO AND PERU
The Aztecs of Mexico and Incas of Peru meted out the death penalty for lesbianism and transvestism. The accused was dragged through town, then burnt.

2. EUROPE, eleventh century
By the eleventh century, the "sin" of oral intercourse was considered serious, and offenders were referred to the bishop. Parish priests only dealt with homosexuality between women under twenty-five, homosexuality between boys under fourteen, and solitary masturbation.

3. FRANCE, thirteenth century
Female sodomy, first and second offense: Mutilation
Third offense: Death by fire

4. HOLY ROMAN EMPIRE, sixteenth century
The *Constitutio Criminalis* of Charles V prescribed death by fire for female sodomy.

5. SPAIN, sixteenth century
Flirting and courting: Public denouncement
Genital rubbing: Public beating
Penetration or use of a dildo: Death

6. AMERICAN COLONIES, seventeenth century
In 1656, New Haven Colony adopted Rev. John Cotton's sodomy law, which prescribed the death penalty for idolatry and blasphemy, breaking the Sabbath, witchcraft, masturbation, and sodomy. The statute charged that sodomy turned the natural use of sexuality into that which was against nature.

7. ENGLAND, nineteenth century
The punishment for homosexual acts was changed from death to prison in 1861. However, there was no mention of lesbianism

in English law.

Legend holds that the law specifically omitted acts of lesbian sex because no one could bear to bring up the dread word in Queen Victoria's presence.

Another version is that when the matter *was* brought up, Victoria — a prude of the most outrageous sort whose era was known for covering piano legs out of modesty to "feminine sensibility," while having the highest rate of prostitution in the history of the nation — not only professed ignorance of the phenomenon but refused to believe such acts between women could possibly take place.

8. GERMANY, nineteenth century

Paragraph 175 of the German Penal Code outlawed homosexual acts between men but did not mention lesbian acts between women.

9. UNITED STATES, twentieth century

In 1939, the Georgia Supreme Court ruled that sodomy cannot take place between two women. The 1986 Hardwick decision overturned this.

10. NEW ZEALAND, twentieth century

In 1988, New Zealand decided that the foreign lovers of lesbian and gay men can apply for residency if they can show a stable relationship of at least four years' duration.

In England that same year, Christine Moss, an Australian who had lived with her lesbian lover for five years, was told that she could not use her relationship as a basis for a residency permit and had to leave England.

13 Women Punished for Lesbian Acts or Cross-Dressing

1. ANONYMOUS, 1536, France

The first recorded instance of such punishment in Europe took place in France. A woman from Fontaine was burned at the stake for impersonating a man. She was accused of marrying a woman and using a dildo for "unnatural sexual intercourse."

2. ANONYMOUS, 1580, Italy

In his journal of a trip to Italy, Montaigne recorded the case of a weaver being executed for lesbian sex acts in that year.

3. MLLE. DE MAUPIN, seventeenth century, France

A singer who played male roles, de Maupin ran off with a rich merchant's daughter while on tour. When the girl realized Maupin was a woman, she left her and informed the authorities of her true sex. Maupin was condemned to death and imprisoned, but due to her great popularity, her sentence was overturned as she awaited execution. When released, she returned to the stage and continued to wear men's clothes, offstage and on.

4. ELIZABETH JOHNSON, 1642, Massachusetts

A servant, Johnson was whipped and fined for "unseemly practices" between herself and another maid in the Bay Colony.

5. & 6. SARA NORMAN and MARY HAMMON, 1649, American colonies

Norman, a married woman, and her lover Hammon were charged with "lewd conduct upon a bed." Because of her youth — 15 years — charges against Norman were dropped. Hammon was let off with a warning but had to publicly acknowledge "unchaste behavior" before the Plymouth Bay Colony.

7. CATHARINE LINCK, 1721, Germany

A cross-dresser, Linck had served as a soldier in the German, Polish, and Russian armies. She eventually settled down and married a woman. But after a fight with Linck, the distraught wife told her mother who, in turn, exposed Linck.

Linck was burned at the stake. Part of the evidence used

against her was a leather dildo she had devised for sexual uses.

8. MARY "GEORGE" HAMILTON, 1746, England

Hamilton was convicted of transvestism and use of a dildo. She had been married at least three times and when she was exposed, she was publicly whipped in a number of different towns and then imprisoned.

9. ANNE "JEAN BAPTISTE" GRANDJEAN, eighteenth century, France

Raised as a boy, Grandjean was so insistent upon passing as a man that she got the town priest to change her name. She married a woman who claimed not to know Jean Baptiste was female until an ex-lover of Jean's told her.

Upon discovery, Grandjean was put in stocks and imprisoned. On her release, she was prohibited from wearing men's clothes.

10. HENRICA SCHURIA, eighteenth century, France

Although she cross-dressed and served as a soldier in the French army, Schuria did not attempt to pass as a man once she left the military. But she did continue to be a lesbian and got involved with a widow who was so satisfied with Schuria that, at Schuria's trial, she said she would have gladly married her if she could.

However, the townspeople were not so enamoured of Schuria as her paramour. When the affair was discovered, Schuria was whipped with rods and then banished.

11. ELLA THOMPSON, 1939, U.S.

Thompson was arrested for lesbianism, tried, and released when the Georgia Supreme Court ruled that sodomy cannot be accomplished between two women.

The law was later changed to make oral sex between two women an act of sodomy in that state.

12. & 13. MARY YOUNG and DAWN DE BLANC, 1967, U.S.

Even though Young and De Blanc may have been prostitutes entrapped by police for "giving a show," they were sentenced to thirty months in prison for crimes against nature.

On appeal, the Louisiana Supreme Court ruled that oral sex between two women constituted "unnatural carnal copulation."

10 Women from the U.S. Military Who Faced Court-Martial, Discharge, or Imprisonment for Allegedly Being Gay

Witch hunts of lesbians seem far away today — unless the women are in the military. Then it is a fact of everyday life and a threat which hangs over every woman's head.

Military witch hunts occur with striking regularity. In the years following World War II, numerous lesbians were drummed out of the service. Twenty women were discharged from the Navy in 1953. They were roused from their beds in the middle of the night, taken in for questioning, and booted out.

In 1980, one-quarter of the women aboard the *U.S.S. Norton Sound* were investigated. Eight were discharged. Half of the sixteen women originally accused were black and charges of racism were raised during the case.

In 1988, a witchhunt of lesbians at the Parris Island Marine Recruit Depot in South Carolina led to the investigation of at least forty women.

Recent statistics from the Department of Defense Advisory Committee on Women in the Services reveal that lesbians in the military are three times more likely to be hunted down and discharged for being gay than are men.

1. FANNIE CLACKUM, U.S. Air Force, 1952

Clackum was discharged on January 22, 1952. After numerous appeals to the military, she took her case to the U.S. Court of Claims, a civil court, which in 1960 found her dishonorable discharge and severance of pay invalid.

During the investigation Clackum, like most others, said she was never informed of the charges against her, although she was told that some action would probably be taken.

2. MIRIAM BEN-SHALOM, U.S. Army, 1976

Sergeant ben-Shalom was discharged from the Army after

stating she was gay. She has fought for her right to re-enlist under the First Amendment right of free speech and the Fifth Amendment right of equal protection. In 1988, the Seventh Circuit Court of Appeals in Chicago ruled that the military could not ban her from the service because she is a lesbian.

3. & 4. WENDI WILLIAMS and ALICIA HARRIS, U.S. Navy, 1980

Williams and Harris were two of the black women investigated in the *U.S.S. Norton Sound* witchhunt. Although found guilty of homosexual behavior, both were given honorable discharges.

5. BARBARA BAUM, U.S. Marines, 1988

A Marine corporal, Baum was sentenced to one year's imprisonment for alleged acts of "sodomy, indecent acts and conspiring to obstruct justice."

Because of protests from the lesbian and gay community as well as veteran's groups, Baum was granted clemency and did not serve the full year. At press time, she was fighting the dishonorable discharge and reduction in rank.

6. LAURA HINCKLEY, U.S. Marines, 1988

Although Hinckley was one of the first women to enter the U.S. Naval Academy and graduated in the top fifteen percent of her class, she faced a general court-martial for fraternizing with Barbara Baum.

7. TERRY KNOX, U.S. Navy, 1988

Petty Officer Knox was charged with perjury after denying statements made about an alleged romance with Marine Sergeant Mary Kile. During interrogation, Knox was allegedly told she could lose custody of her child if she didn't cooperate.

8. MARY KILE, U.S. Marines, 1988

Sergeant Kile was charged with perjury when she recanted testimony against other women made after eight hours of interrogation by the Naval Investigative Service, during which she was allegedly denied legal counsel. She faced charges of fraternization and indecent acts.

9. CHERYL JAMESON, U. S. Marines, 1988

Jameson served time in the brig for obstruction of justice as well as indecent acts even though she was an outstanding drill instructor with a top security clearance. Although she had ten years' service, she was stripped of rank and retirement benefits.

Jameson is one of the many black women who are being drummed out of the military in this purge.

10. CINDY MORAN, U.S. Air Force, 1988

Airman Moran was court-martialed at MacDill Air Force Base in Florida for allegedly kissing a woman who spent the night at her home during tropical storm Keith. Moran says she is wrongly accused and is fighting the charges.

3 Lesbians Fighting for Security Clearance

1. MARGARET A. PADULA

In the 1987 case "Padula v. Webster," United States Court of Appeals for the District of Columbia, Padula had to fight for a right to work at the Federal Bureau of Investigation because she was a lesbian. The FBI declined to hire her even though she scored well on admissions tests. She took them to court, arguing that a policy of discrimination against homosexuals created a "suspect classification."

2. JEAN KOVALICH

Kovalich settled an anti-discrimination suit at the Defense Investigative Service. She was given back her supervisory post and received back pay.

3. JULIE DUBBS

Dubbs has filed suit against the Central Intelligence Agency for discrimination because she was denied a security clearance necessary to her job. A technical illustrator for a defense contractor, Dubbs had applied for a clearance in 1981 and been denied it. As a homosexual, the CIA said, she was "exploitable."

In early 1989, the U.S. Court of Appeals, Ninth Circuit, found that the CIA's policy of denying security clearances to lesbians and gay men constituted unacceptable discrimination. This opened the way for Dubbs's lawsuit against the CIA.

7 Lesbian Murderers and Accused Murderers

1. ALICE MITCHELL

In 1892, nineteen-year-old Alice Mitchell jumped from a carriage and slit the throat of seventeen-year-old Freda "Fred" Ward. Mitchell, the daughter of a wealthy Memphis merchant, killed Ward when the two were forbidden to see each other or to say the other's name.

Mitchell claimed that she could not live without Ward, the daughter of a planter. She said that they had made a compact that if they were ever separated, they should kill each other.

At one point, Mitchell and Ward had exchanged engagement rings but when Ward returned her ring to Mitchell, Mitchell allegedly resolved to kill her.

2. NETTIE MILLER

Hattie Leonard lived with Nettie Miller for fourteen years, during which time Leonard had left on numerous occasions, claiming Miller had assaulted her for "accepting the attentions of a drug store clerk." When Leonard finally married, Miller shot the man.

3. LIZZIE BORDEN

Although many people have heard songs and stories about Lizzie Borden, few people know that she also had a love affair with Nance O'Neill. Borden was accused of killing her father and stepmother with an ax. She pleaded innocent and was eventually acquitted but her name — and her deed — lives on.

4. THE PAPIN SISTERS

These two French sisters, who were alleged to be lovers, were also employed together as servants. They were charged with turning on their employer, murdering the wife and daughter while the distraught husband stood by in helpless shock. The cult film *Les Abysse*, by Nico Papatakis, is based on this story.

5. SUSAN SAXE

Saxe pleaded guilty to a lesser charge at a trial for a 1970 bank robbery that included felony murder. Her first trial had ended with a hung jury; the second was heard by a "hanging judge" and she was imprisoned. Her lover, Byrna Aronson, was banned from the courtroom for "outbursts" during the trial.

6. & 7. SARA MAE RICHARDSON and LYNN PFENDER

Although their actions pale beside contemporary serial murders, these two lovers were believed to be in the habit of picking up men in parks, taking them for rides, stealing their clothes, and dumping them in the buff.

In 1984, they were accused of shooting two Turkish students, one of whom died. The women turned themselves in.

6 Odd Brushes with the Law

1. AUGUSTA MAIN

In 1897 Miss Augusta Main, spinster farmer of Berlin, New York, was held on one thousand dollars bail for assaulting a male neighbor with intent to kill. Miss Main did all the farm work herself and allowed no men on the premises. When needing extra hands at harvest time, she hired "strapping young women."

In her defense, Miss Main said she "never sees men or dogs but what she aches to kill them."

2. EVA LE GALLIENNE

An actress, Le Gallienne was named in a 1930 alienation of affection lawsuit filed by a New York socialite against his wife, Josephine Hutchinson. During the trial, the husband stated that Josephine preferred the company of Le Gallienne "Morning, noon and night."

3. & 4. PATRICIA "MIZMOON" SOLTYSIK and CAMILLA HALL

When the Symbionese Liberation Army gained national attention by kidnapping Patty Hearst, the daughter of one of the wealthiest newspaper publishers in the U.S., these two lesbians made headlines as members of the group.

Hall and Soltysik had met prior to joining the SLA, and the *San Francisco Chronicle* published love poems from Hall to Mizmoon during the 1974 media blitz on the subject. They were killed that year when the Los Angeles house where they made a last stand was torched by a S.W.A.T. team.

5. Z BUDAPEST

An avowed lesbian witch, Z Budapest was arrested in 1975 for fortune-telling when she did a tarot reading for an undercover policewoman. At the time, Budapest claimed that not one law enforcement officer touched her during the arrest because she threatened to hex the first person who did with nightmares.

She was convicted of the offense but tried to get her case appealed in the hope of seeing all U.S. laws against witchcraft —

and the traditional ways witches make a living — revoked.

6. SISTER MARY KREGAR

In a 1988 judgment, Sister Mary Kregar, a Catholic nun, was ordered to pay one million dollars damages to Steve Woolverton of Brownsville, Texas, for seducing his wife and destroying his marriage. Woolverton argued that his wife's joining the Brownsville Catholic Diocese choir apparently led to the breach.

The Church was also directed to pay five hundred thousand dollars for negligence even though it had dismissed Kregar after learning of the affair. Kregar left the Franciscan order in August 1984 and became a social worker. Defense attorneys said that the lawsuit was a ploy on Woolverton's part for money.

6 *Lesbian Custody Cases*

Married women who come out often face the prospect of losing their children. While many women are winning these battles, the financial and psychic costs are still high.

1. ROSALIE DAVIES
In a typical case, Davies lost custody of her children in 1972 after leaving her husband. Davies had had affairs with women all of her married life but it was only after she and her husband divorced that lesbianism became an issue. Not one to give up easily, Davies enrolled in law school that year and eventually founded Custody Action for Lesbian Mothers (CALM).

2. JEANNE JULLION
In 1977, Jullion lost custody of her two sons to her ex-husband, an attorney who had abducted the youngest boy before the case was heard. Prior to the trial, Jullion lived with her lover and her lover's four children in what's now called a blended family. Jullion's eldest son already lived with the father. Ironically, Jullion's attempt to gain custody of the eldest led to her losing both.

3. KATHY RILEY
That same year, Riley, a black lesbian, won custody of her deceased lover's daughter, in a precedent-setting case.

4. MARGARETH MILLER
Miller regained custody of her daughter in 1979 after the Michigan Supreme Court reversed a lower-court ruling against her. The decision is thought to be the first time a court ruled in favor of a gay parent by saying that the parent's sexuality should have no bearing on their child-rearing abilities.

5. MARGARET WALES
Wales was not so lucky. In this instance, the judge felt it would be in the best interests of her two daughters to live with their

father rather than their lesbian mother and her lover. Wales lost custody in the early 1980s.

6. SHARON BROWN

In a somewhat complicated case, Brown lost a 1989 custody battle to her grandparents, who had been taking care of her son since birth because Brown was a cocaine addict. Brown had since undergone treatment but when she tried to get her son back, her grandparents filed for custody and won.

3 Lesbian-Lesbian Custody Battles

With the increasing use of artificial insemination by lesbians wanting children, the non-biological mothers in lesbian couples are finding that they have few legal rights if the two women break up. The same holds true for couples who adopt children with only one woman going through the legal process.

1. ANGELA CURIALE

Curiale's daughter, Alexandra, was four when Curiale and her lover broke up. A senior psychologist and teacher, Curiale claimed to have supported her lover during the artificially-inseminated pregnancy and once the child was born.

After the end of their five-year relationship, Curiale stated that she signed over their jointly-owned home. But, according to Curiale, once her lover got the deed to the house, she refused to let Curiale see the child.

When Curiale took the matter to court, she lost. She has vowed to take the case as far as necessary to see her daughter again.

2. TERRI SABOL

Although Sabol's lover bore a child by artificial insemination, Sabol hoped to create an emotional, biological, and legal bond by using a donation from one of her own male relatives. Courts have generally refused to hear custody cases between biological and non-biological lesbian mothers, but in early 1989 Sabol was granted permission by the Los Angeles Superior Court to seek joint custody of her two-year-old.

3. DENISE WHEELER

According to Wheeler, she and her lover agreed as a couple to adopt a ten-hour-old girl in 1980, though her lover was the one who actually went through the adoption process. When the two women broke up, they shared joint custody until 1985 when the daughter disappeared from her day-care center in California.

Wheeler tracked her ex-lover and daughter to another state. She filed for suit in California, hoping to have the case tried there because she hoped the court would be more liberal. But she could not get the California courts to recognize her custodial rights and accept jurisdiction over the case.

11 Acts of Censorship

1. IN 1900, OLGA NETHERSOLE WAS ARRESTED for giving an indecent performance in the New York version of *Sapho*. The play was closed until Nethersole was acquitted.

2. POLICE BANNED THE 1907 MOULIN ROUGE performance of *Rêve D'Égypte* when Colette's lover "Missy," the Marquise de Belbeuf, joined her on stage to act the male lead, Yssim. The play ended with the two women kissing.

3. IN 1917, DR. MARY EDWARDS WALKER'S NAME was removed from the list of Congressional Medal of Honor winners for "undisclosed" reasons. Walker — a surgeon who wore a man's first-lieutenant uniform in the Union Army and had been granted permission to do so by a special act of Congress — had been awarded the medal by President Andrew Johnson in 1866.

4. IN 1922, THE WHOLE BROADWAY CAST of *The God of Vengeance*, which had a lesbian couple at the center of the drama, was arrested when the New York Grand Jury indicted them for presenting an "immoral and impure" theatrical production. But that hardly stopped the play. The actors paid the bail and were back for the matinee the next day. The New York state penal code had been amended in 1909 specifically to add "sexual degeneracy and perversion" to the obscenity laws. As a result, playhouse doors could be padlocked for a year in punishment, which effectively prohibited Broadway plays from dealing with lesbians or gay men in any but the most subtle and underhanded way. The statute wasn't removed from the books until 1967.

5. IN A SENSATIONAL POLICE RAID, the cast of *The Captive* was arrested in New York on February 9, 1927. The drama played five more days before the cast was charged with corrupting morality and the play closed. Prior to the U.S. debacle, it had been seen in Paris, Brussels, Berlin, Vienna, and other European capitals. It was also banned in San Francisco, Los Angeles, Detroit,

Budapest, and London. Ironically, the day before the New York arrest, producer and director Gilbert Miller had been awarded the Legion of Honor in France.

6. THE LESBIAN CHARACTER OF COUNTESS GESCHWITZ was removed from the original U.S. film version of G.W. Pabst's 1929 movie, *Pandora's Box.* The scenes were later restored.

Movies were particularly hard hit by censors. In 1915, the U.S. Supreme Court ruled that movies were not part of the press or organs of public opinion but a business. As such, they constituted entertainment and were not covered by the First Amendment. Seven years later, thirty-two states had passed their own censorship laws. These laws were specifically directed at gay characters and were so effective that the mere threat of lawsuits kept many producers from attempting to include them in stories.

In 1930, the movie industry itself instituted the Motion Picture Production Code. The code came to be known as the "Hays Code," after the Presbyterian elder from Indiana who headed the Motion Picture Producers and Distributors of America for many years. Hays was responsible for the insertion of a morals clause into the contracts of many actors and actresses, which meant that any deviation from the norm could result in their immediate ouster from the studio at a time when the major studios had an iron grip on the industry.

The Code also ensured that lesbians and gay men weren't portrayed in a positive light. If seen at all, they were seen as decadent and degenerate. In the rare cases when they were portrayed in a more sympathetic light, they still "got theirs" in the end.

The Code was not revised until 1956.

7. FEAR OF THE CODE WAS SO SUCCESSFUL that the original U.S. version of the movie *Mädchen in Uniform* was cut to suit the Hays office. Lesbian references were deleted — in a film that relied on lesbianism for its plot. The censorship was so successful that Bland Johnson, a critic for the New York *Mirror*, wrote in 1932 that "it is a simple, clean, wholesome little tale of schoolgirl crushes."

8. IN THE 1933 MOVIE *QUEEN CHRISTINA*, Garbo as Christina was turned into a heterosexual with only hints of lesbianism. Since Christina actually abdicated the throne rather than marry and bear an heir, this constituted a major rewriting of history.

9. THE 1936 VERSION OF LILLIAN HELLMAN'S PLAY *The Children's Hour* was reduced to a love triangle by director William Wyler, who retitled it *These Three*. The producer, Sam Goldwyn, wanted to leave the play's original lesbian couple intact but had been told by the Hays Office that it wouldn't lift the ban on lesbianism even if the subject were handled in a tasteful way.

10. IN 1968, THE SEDUCTION SCENE from the movie *The Killing of Sister George* was cut in several states where it violated local obscenity laws.

11. IN THE AUSTRALIAN MOVIE *MY BRILLIANT CAREER*, no mention was made of the fact that in real life, Sybylla, the heroine, didn't marry because she was a lesbian. Instead, her reason for remaining single was never mentioned.

6 Banned Lesbian Books
and Works of Art

Although we usually think of book burnings as a thing of the past, the practice is alive and well today. Banned lesbian writers join a long list of distinguished authors — from Sappho to John Steinbeck and J.D. Salinger.

1. THE BANNING OF SAPPHO'S POEMS throughout the centuries is the most telling example of heterosexual censorship. Although Sappho was the most acclaimed poet of her day, only a twentieth of her output has survived what is euphemistically called "the ravages of time."

Her work was first burned by Christians during the purge of the great library at Alexandria around A.D. 390, because it was considered pagan. Works that survived were publicly burnt by order of Pope Gregory VII in the late eleventh century. Only one poem, and that brief, has survived in its entirety.

As if that weren't enough, her poems were systematically translated using heterosexual imagery until the 1925 Miller-and-Robinson translation that acknowledges the women Sappho wrote to. Prior to that, translators took the liberty of changing love objects from "she" to "he."

Her love life was also heavily censored until recently, as critics tried to find a man in her life. A ferryman some thirty years younger was invented as a possible lover, to avoid dealing with her true orientation.

2. IN 1925, ROMAINE BROOKS'S PORTRAIT of Lady Una Troubridge, in tuxedo and monocle, was banned from a show of her paintings in London.

3. IN 1929, RADCLYFFE HALL'S NOVEL *The Well of Loneliness* was the object of two seizures. Police in England seized 247 copies while police in the U.S. took 865.

Two drawn-out censorship battles ensued. In both cases,

judges felt that the book would corrupt public morals and it was banned. The English judgment was upheld on appeal but the U.S. verdict was overturned.

Despite their surface similarity, the two cases were quite different. The English censorship — and the vituperative personal attacks which preceded it — came as a surprise to Hall. In the U.S., however, the publishers were prepared for an onslaught and used the seizure of the books to good advantage in a publicity campaign.

All the same, the allegations and attacks hurt Hall enormously. She fled England soon after the first trial and didn't return for years. Whatever the personal cost, the trials ensured maximum publicity on both sides of the Atlantic. As a result, sales of the book took off.

4. IN 1984, DJUNA BARNES'S NOVEL *RYDER* was seized by British customs on the grounds of obscenity.

5. IN 1989, ARTIST CATHY PHILLIPS was charged with an "obscene expression in a public place" for her sculpture of a bedroom and bed. At the foot of the bed were the words: "She ran her tongue like fire across my nipples. She slipped her hand in my cunt and grinned."

In her defense, Phillips said she was tired of people assuming that art was heterosexual and that she wanted to celebrate her relationship with her lover. The sculpture was in a public park in Melbourne, Australia.

6. BECAUSE OF HER POLITICS, Pat Califia has had repeated run-ins with censors. In 1982, her book *Sapphistry: The Book of Lesbian Sex* was removed from the recommended text list for classes at California State University, Long Beach. In 1984, it was shredded by British customs. In 1989, *Macho Sluts* was impounded by Canadian Customs.

What 9 Newspapers, Magazines, and Individuals Said about *"The Well of Loneliness"*

Radclyffe Hall was a moderately successful mainstream novelist when, encouraged by her lover, Lady Una Troubridge, to write the "true story" of a lesbian's life, she wrote *The Well of Loneliness*. Hall expected some censure over the sympathetic treatment of homosexuality in the book but was completely unprepared for the furor which ensued.

During the months following publication, Hall's private life — and her penchant for cross-dressing — was brutally satirized. A photograph of her in drag was spread across the Sunday papers.

Hall chose to base her book on the "nature" argument — that lesbians can't help it because they are born that way. While this was a useful tactic in eliciting sympathy from the general public, it offended many lesbians of the day who had rejected the heterosexual route and were proud of their sexuality.

1. "If Christianity does not destroy this doctrine, then this doctrine will destroy it, together with civilization. I would rather give a healthy boy or girl a phial of prussic acid than this novel."
   —James Douglas, *Sunday Express*, Aug. 19, 1928.

2. "There is not one word which suggests that anyone with the horrible tendencies described is in the least blameworthy."
   —Sir Chartres Biron, Magistrate for the English obscenity trial, *London Times*, Nov. 17, 1928.

3. "The normal must be kept from knowledge of the invert lest the latter infect the former."
   —Robert Morss Lovett, *New Republic*, Jan. 2, 1929.

4. It is "worthwhile to call public attention to the badly misunderstood plight of many, many men and women."
— *Nation*, January 1929.

5. "Even our syncopated music has become more so — super-
syncopated. The jungle and the savage strive to force themselves into our existence and the age of boundless hilarity and
orgies has set in."
— Dr. Noah E. Aronstam,
in a medical journal, August 1929.

6. A "ridiculous, trite, superficial book."
— Romaine Brooks, quoted in *Between Me and Life:
A Biography of Romaine Brooks*, by Meryle Secrest.

7. "A loathsome example."
— Violet Trefusis, letter to Vita Sackville-West,
quoted in *The Other Woman: The Life of Violet Trefusis*,
by Philippe Julian and John Phillips.

8. "A Lesbian Bible."
— Del Martin, *Lesbian/Woman*, 1972.

9. "*The Well of Loneliness* may have been misunderstood."
— *Woman's Journal*, in a review of Hall's next book,
The Unlit Lamp, October 1929.

"Pray to God, dear. She will help you."
— Emmeline Pankhurst, English suffragist

6 Individuals Who Weren't Allowed to Testify on Radclyffe Hall's Behalf

Prior to publication in England of *The Well of Loneliness*, a three-month campaign by the press to suppress the book had been so successful that the trial was a sham. Emotion ran so high that no one was allowed to testify on Hall's behalf. Noted here are six of many willing to do so.

1. VIRGINIA WOOLF, literary critic, novelist, and lover of Vita Sackville-West

2. LEONARD WOOLF, essayist, publisher, and husband of Virginia Woolf

3. VITA SACKVILLE-WEST, lesbian aristocrat and author

4. E.M. FORSTER, closeted gay novelist and author of *Maurice*

5. DESMOND McCARTHY, literary critic

6. SIR JULIAN HUXLEY, noted biologist and brother of author Aldous Huxley

6 Individuals
Who Were Allowed to Testify*

The book was also tried in the U.S., but the trial was used as part of a clever publicity campaign. Seventy-four Americans testified on the book's behalf, including:

1. ERNEST HEMINGWAY, novelist

2. JOHN DOS PASSOS, novelist

3. EDNA FERBER, novelist

4. SINCLAIR LEWIS, novelist

5. SHERWOOD ANDERSON, playwright

6. THEODORE DREISER, whose own book, *An American Tragedy*, had been judged obscene two years earlier.

*This list and the previous one are based on information in *Woman Plus Woman*, by Dolores Klaich.

A Global Affair

13 Cities with Lesbian Archives

1. BERLIN

2. BOLOGNA

3. BRUSSELS

4. COPENHAGEN

5. HELSINKI

6. LONDON

7. LOS ANGELES

8. NEW YORK

9. PARIS

10. ROME

11. SAN FRANCISCO

12. STOCKHOLM

13. WELLINGTON, New Zealand

17 Dutch Lesbians *

1. CATHARINA ALBERDINGK THIJM, b. 1849, nineteenth-century writer

2. JOANNA CRAMER, married to cross-dressing soldier Maria van Antwerpen in 1748

3. PIA BECK, b. 1925, twentieth-century jazz singer and pianist

4. BET VAN BEEREN, b. 1902, café owner who was called "the Queen of the Zeedijk," a famous street in the center of Amsterdam.

5. FRIEDA BELINFANTE, early twentieth-century cellist

6. ANNA BLAMAN, 1905-1960, pseudonym of early twentieth-century poet and writer, Johanna Petronella Vrugt. In 1948, she wrote the first lesbian novel published in the Netherlands, which caused a tremendous scandal. *Eenzaam Avontuur* is her most famous book

7. MARIE DE BOER, an early twentieth-century nurse who was the first lesbian to sign the homosexual rights petition of 1911

8. HENRIËTTE BOSMANS, b. 1895, early twentieth-century composer and pianist

9. TIL BRUGMAN, b. 1888, writer and lover of German artist, Hannah Höch

10. ANDREAS BURNIER, b. 1931, pseudonym of Dr. C.I. Dessaur, professor of criminology and contemporary essayist

11. TON DANEN, therapist and board member of Cultuur en Ontspannings-Centrum (COC), which was founded in 1946

and is believed to be the oldest existing gay and lesbian organization in the world.

12. AAGJE DEKEN, 1741-1804, author; wrote *Sara Burgerhardt* with her housemate Betje Wolff. Deken was also one of the earliest women's rights activists.

13. EVELIEN ESHUIS, b. 1942, first openly lesbian member of the Dutch Parliament, and a member of the Communist Party.

14. ANNEMARIE GREWEL, b. 1935, member of the City Council of Amsterdam, former chairperson of the Council of Amsterdam University, and professor of science

15. KAAT MOSSEL, b. 1723, political activist who was also known as Caetje Mulder. She was a favorite of Willem van Orange and was romantic friends with Cornelia Swenke

16. JOSINE REULING, b. 1899; writer and author of *Return of the Island* (1936), a relatively explicit lesbian book

17. JACOBA SURIE, b. 1879; painter and member of "De Amsterdamse Joffers," a group of eight female painters

*Courtesy of Judith Schuyf, Interfacultaire Werkgroep Homostudies, Rijksuniversiteit te Utrecht and Renee van de Giessen, International Lesbian Information Service, Amsterdam.

5 Swedish Lesbians *

1. KARIN BOYE, 1900-1941
Like many homosexuals of the time, Boye went to live in the liberated city of Berlin during the gay heyday before Hitler came to power. She committed suicide during World War II, ending a superb literary career. Today, despite the short span of her life, Boye is numbered among Sweden's finest poets.

2. QUEEN CHRISTINA, b. 1626
Although known for abdicating the Swedish throne rather than live a lifestyle she did not want, Christina is also remembered in her native land for converting to Catholicism in later life and inviting Descartes to Stockholm. Not her fault that he died there of pneumonia.

3. KLARA JOHANSSON
Johansson is a twentieth-century literary critic and author well known for her essays.

4. SELMA LAGERLÖF, 1858-1940
A Nobel Prize laureate and the first woman admitted to the prestigious Swedish Academy, Lagerlöf wrote many novels in the late nineteenth and early twentieth centuries. She had a lifelong romantic friendship with author Sophie Elkan.

5. ANNE CHARLOTTE EDGREN-LEFFLER, b. 1849
A realistic novelist and dramatist, Leffler's short stories include *The Actress, The Family,* and *A Rescuing Angel.* She also wrote books with her intimate friend, Russian novelist Sonya Kovalevsky, who was a mathematics professor at the University of Stockholm for many years.

*Courtesy of Jens Rydström, International Lesbian and Gay Association, Stockholm.

7 German Lesbians *

1. ANITA AUGSPURG, 1857-1943, late nineteenth- and early twentieth-century radical suffragist and romantic friend of Lida Gustava Heymann

2. ANITA BERBER, b. 1899, dancer and actress

3. LIDA GUSTAVA HEYMANN, 1868-1943, radical feminist who wrote the memoir *Erlebtes-Erschautes* with romantic friend Anita Augspurg

4. HANNAH HÖCH, b. 1889, painter and lover of Dutch writer, Til Brugman

5. GERTRUDE SANDMAN, b. 1893, painter

6. RENÉE SINTENIS, b. 1800, sculptor

7. CLAIRE WALDOFF, b. 1884, singer

*Courtesy of Spinnboden Lesbenarchiv, Berlin.

11 English Lesbians *

1. PAT ARROWSMITH, contemporary peace activist

2. SARAH BAYLIS, twentieth-century writer

3. LINDA BELLOS, contemporary politician

4. FRANCES POWER COBBE, 1822-1904, nineteenth-century women's rights activist

5. MAUREEN COLQUHOUN, contemporary politician

6. EDY CRAIG, twentieth-century theater producer and designer

7. EMILY FAITHFULL, 1835-1895, nineteenth-century printer and activist

8. JACKIE FORSTER, twentieth-century lesbian rights activist

9. SOPHIA JEX-BLAKE, nineteenth-century doctor and women's rights advocate

10. ROSEMARY MANNING, twentieth-century writer

11. MIRIAM MARGOLYES, twentieth-century actress

*Courtesy of the Lesbian Archive and Information Centre, London.

6 Lesbian Writers and Artists From Asia

In many parts of Asia, homosexuality has long been considered another part of human nature. This was especially true in Japan, China, and Thailand. But because of the sexist nature of these ancient societies, little is known of women of the past, less so of lesbians.

1. YOSANO AKIKO, poet

2. OTAKE KUOKICHI, painter

3. HIRAZUKA RAICHO, writer

4. YAMAKAWA TOMIKO, author

5. WU TSAO, poet

6. MIAMOTO YURIKO, writer

"My life is an archive."
                    Theresa Corrigan, owner of Lioness Books

Bibliography

Ackroyd, Peter, *Dressing Up: Transvestism and Drag; The History of an Obsession.* New York: Simon & Schuster, 1979.

Boughner, Terry, *Out of All Time.* Boston: Alyson Publications, 1988.

Budapest, Z, *The Feminist Book of Lights and Shadows.* Los Angeles: Luna Publications, 1976.

Butler, Iris, *The Great Duchess: The Life of Sarah Churchill.* New York: Funk & Wagnalls, 1967.

Cavin, Susan, *Lesbian Origins.* San Francisco: Ism Press, 1985.

Cook, Blanche Wiesen, *Female Support Networks and Political Activism.* Los Angeles: *Chrysalis* magazine, 1977.

Corinne, Tee, *Women Who Loved Women.* Portland: Pearlchild, 1984.

Cowan, Thomas, *Gay Men and Women Who Enriched the World.* New Canaan: Mulvey Books, 1988.

Curtin, Kaier, *We Can Always Call Them Bulgarians.* Boston: Alyson Publications, 1987.

Daly, Mary, *Gyn/Ecology: the Metaethics of Radical Feminism.* Boston: Beacon Press, 1978.

Dekker, Rudolf M., and Lotte C. van de Pol, *the Tradition of Female Transvestism in Early Modern Europe.* New York: St. Martin's Press, 1989.

Diner, Helen, *Mothers and Amazons.* New York: Anchor Press, 1973.

Ehrenpreis, Irvin, and Robert Halsband, *The Lady of Letters in the Eighteenth Century.* Los Angeles: University of California, 1969.

Ehrenreich, Barbara, and Deirdre English, *Witches, Midwives and Nurses: A History of Women Healers.* New York: Feminist Press, 1973.

Faber, Doris, *The Life of Lorena Hickok, E.R.'s Friend*. New York: William Morrow, 1980.

Faderman, Lillian, *Surpassing the Love of Men*. New York: William Morrow, 1981.

_____, and Brigitte Eriksson, *Lesbian-Feminism in Turn-of-the-Century Germany*. Tallahassee: Naiad Press, 1980.

Figes, Eva, *Patriarchal Attitudes*. Greenwich: Fawcett Publications, 1970.

Foster, Jeannette A., *Sex Variant Women in Literature*. Tallahassee: Naiad, 1985.

Fraser, Antonia, *The Warrior Queens*. New York: Alfred A. Knopf, 1989.

Fraser, Sir James G., *The Golden Bough*. New York: Macmillan, 1922.

Freedman, Hy, *Sex Link*. New York: M. Evans, 1977.

Grahn, Judy, *Another Mother Tongue: Gay Words, Gay Worlds*. Boston: Beacon Press, 1984.

_____, *The Highest Apple*. San Francisco: Spinsters Ink, 1985.

Greif, Martin, *The Gay Book of Days*. Secaucus: Lyle Stuart, 1982.

Grier, Barbara, *The Lesbian in Literature*. Tallahassee: Naiad Press, 1981.

Hepburn, Cuca, and Bonnie Gutierrez, *Alive and Well: A Lesbian Health Guide*. Freedom, Calif.: Crossing Press, 1988.

Hull, Gloria, Patricia Bell Scott, and Barbara Smith, *But Some of Us Are Brave*. New York: Feminist Press, 1982.

International Lesbian and Gay Association, *Second ILGA Pink Book*. Utrecht: Interfacultaire Werkgroep Homostudies, Rijksuniversiteit Utrecht, 1988.

Katz, Jonathan Ned, *Gay American History*. New York: Avon, 1976.

_____, *Gay/Lesbian Almanac*. New York: Harper & Row, 1983.

Klaich, Dolores, *Woman Plus Woman*. Tallahassee: Naiad Press, 1989.

Lust, John, *The Herb Book*. New York: Benedict Lust Publications, 1974.

Macfarlane, Alan, *Witchcraft in Tudor and Stuart England*. London: Routledge & Kegan Paul, 1970.

Myron, Nancy, and Charlotte Bunch, *Women Remembered*. Baltimore: Diana Press, 1974.

Navratilova, Martina, *Martina*. New York: Alfred A. Knopf, 1985.

Nicolson, Nigel, *A Portrait of a Marriage*. New York: Atheneum, 1973.

Raymond, Janice G., *A Passion for Friends*. Boston: Beacon Press, 1986.

Rennie, Susan, and Kirsten Grimstad, *The New Woman's Survival Catalogue*. New York: Berkeley Publishing, 1973.

_____, *The New Woman's Survival Sourcebook*. New York: Alfred A. Knopf, 1975.

Roberts, J.R., *Black Lesbians*. Tallahassee: Naiad Press, 1981.

Rodgers, Bruce, *Gay Talk*. New York: Paragon Books, 1972.

Roscoe, Will, *Living the Spirit*. New York: St. Martin's Press, 1988.

Rose, Jeanne, *Herbs and Things*. New York: Workman Publishing, 1972.

Rowbotham, Sheila, *Women, Resistance and Revolution*. Harmondsworth: Penguin Books, 1972.

Russo, Vito, *The Celluloid Closet*. New York: Harper & Row, 1987.

Rutledge, Leigh, *The Gay Book of Lists*. Boston: Alyson Publications, 1987.

Schwarz, Judy, Introduction to *Eye to Eye: Portraits of Lesbians*, by JEB. Washington, D.C.: Glad Hag Books, 1979.

Strachey, Lytton, *Eminent Victorians*. London: Chatto & Windus, 1918.

Sullivan, Louis, *Information for the Female-to-Male Crossdresser and Transsexual*. San Francisco: L. Sullivan, 1985.

Tannahill, Reay, *Sex in History*. New York: Stein & Day, 1980.

Taylor, Kathryn, *Generations of Denial*. New York: Times Change Press, 1971.

Tremain, Rose, *The Fight for Freedom for Women*. New York: Ballantine Books, 1973.

Tyler, Parker, *Screening the Sexes: Homosexuality in the Movies*. New York: Anchor Press, 1972.

Uglow, Jennifer S., *The Macmillan Dictionary of Women's Biographies*. New York: Macmillan, 1982.

Valiente, Doreen, *An ABC of Witchcraft*. New York: St. Martin's Press, 1973.

Vivien, Renée, *A Woman Appeared to Me*. Reno: Naiad Press, 1976.

Wilson, Elizabeth, *Adorned in Dreams: Fashion and Modernity*. London: Virago, 1985.